Why Heal Your Mind, Body, and Spirit? Sleuthing Ways to Love

By Anne M. Logan
Grow Power Self Improvement, LLC

<u>Why Heal Your Mind, Body, and Spirit?</u>
<u>Sleuthing Ways to Love</u>

By Anne M. Logan

For information, post office address:

Grow Power Self Improvement, LLC

Post Office Box 15455

Wilmington, NC 28408

Or

Email: **gps.9339@gmail.com**
Website: **https://www.gpsanne.com**

ISBN-13: 978-1-7325693-0-0

ISBN-10: 17325693-0-4

Library of Congress Control Number:

2018908172

Acknowledgements

This book was written by every dear friend and family member who shared their life secrets, talked, loved, and cried with me. I give a particular thankfulness to Beverly Stone and Naomi Alpern, excellent listeners and dear friends. You are all dear to my heart. I send my love and gratitude.

And

It was Michael, my dear angel, who took me by my hand saying, "Young lady, you're going to write your story about solving your life's difficulties. You will write many books."

This writing is a non-fiction book. However, some fictional names, characters, places, and incidents include as the product of the author's imagination. Any resemblance to actual persons, living or dead, business establishments, events, or locales is entirely coincidental.

Novels

Who Are You? Planned Escape from Abuse

Where Are You? Search for the Truth

Non-Fiction

Why Heal Your Mind, Body, and Spirit?

Sleuthing Ways to Love

Table of Contents

Why Heal Your Mind, Body and Spirit? Sleuthing Ways to Love

'We need to accept that we won't always make the right decision, that we'll screw up royally sometimes – understanding that failure is not the opposite of success, it's part of success.'

Arianna Huffington

Hello My Dear Reader,

Do you feel pain in your mind, body, or spirit? Do you want relief from the negativity? I'm confident you want to release your pain.

What is the definition of your pain? The pain could be from maybe a divorce, a death of a loved one, health problems, injuries from a car accident, work sexual discrimination, or any other traumatic event. As a survivor of the discomfort, you may be experiencing one or more negative emotions such as anger, denial, negativity, guilt, resentment, or sorrow.

How do we heal our negativities? This book will provide information on how to relieve your pain in your mind, body, or spirt; to find your true-life purpose, and to experience the gift of love. I invite you to crawl, walk, run, and fall as you acquire your knowledge of how to heal yourself and find our love for other and self.

As a registered nurse, I discovered how to heal pain in my mind, body, and spirit; and found my true-life purpose, love others and myself. Gaining the understanding of this knowledge, I soon realized the methods included defining a painful life situation, recognizing the difficulties, collecting clues about different challenges, journaling, doing opportunities to manage my stress, discovering love, and finding my multiple true-life purposes.

When we use these healing methods, they are similar to walking on a trail. Sometimes, we may feel lost, take a detour, or turn yet down another unfamiliar path. You invested in this book to heal your mind, body, and spirit; to find your true-life purpose, and to discover love. To achieve a higher level of your healing, I recommend that you write daily either with a pen in your journal or type in your electronic diary. This recommendation will find your love, commitment, confidence, and courage to answer the question, why heal your mind, body, and spirit; to discover your true-life purpose, and to find love for self and others.

Introduction

If you could heal your pain, discover your true-life's purpose, and find love, would you read this book? Yes! Within these pages, you will find your true-life purpose, love, and how to heal your mind, body, and spirit by five manageable strategies. They include 'The Crime, The Slime, The Grime, The Time, and The Prime.'

Using these five unique strategies, the reader will analyze their pain by asking the six questions: who, what, when, where, how, and why. The first strategy, 'The Crime,' is when the individual mourns a painful life event. Anger, is the feature of the second strategy known as 'The Slime,' which is directed towards another person, perhaps themselves, or both. Evaluating and healing the various negative emotions is the third strategy known as 'The Grime.' The 'Time' is learning how to forgive the other person, again ourselves, or both. Finally, 'The Prime,' is seen as we discover love in serving our purpose.

When proceeding through this book, please understand that I've struggled with my healing as you do. I would like to describe my healing process through communicating the lessons learned and sharing my fictional writings, Kate's journal. My healing journey began with writing in my many journals which led to creating Kate, my fictional character.

I discovered that Kate could speak my truth when I was afraid to speak mine. Slowly, Kate's words evolved into writing my two self-published novels, <u>Who Are You? Planned Escape from Abuse</u> and <u>Where Are You? Search for the Truth</u>. If you desire to read more, either go to my website, **www.gpsanne.com** or Amazon books.

Let's turn to focus on how to proceed through this book, <u>Why Heal Your Mind, Body, and Spirit? Sleuthing Ways to Love</u>. When understanding how to manage a chapter, you may pick one or more approaches. They may include reading a section, writing in your diary, participating in one of the different activities, or selecting a healing opportunity chosen from the lists of the mind, body, or spirit.

Follow your intuition to go straight through each chapter, to jump forward to a future one, or to return to a preceding section. Why? Your painful path is not a straight, narrow road; therefore, your healing isn't to follow a traditional path either.

While you are reading this book, you may feel isolated, but realize you are not alone. The reason is that I believe our higher spirits are connected. Shall we continue? Please consider if you want to continue now or later. Thank you.

As we begin this journey, I may be hearing you say, 'I don't have the time to read, ponder, write, or engage in anything more than what I'm currently doing! I'm too busy with caring for my children, assisting my elderly parents, completing my work responsibilities, undertaking my housework, doing my college commitments, etc.'

Yes, I understand that you are overwhelmed with your current life; however, our mutual goals include improving the quality of your life, finding your true-life purpose, and discovering love.

I appreciate that you may not realize that you do not differ from any other woman trying to survive each day's responsibilities. Historically, women worked and lived busy lives as caregivers, and you may fit this role. Understanding our caregiving functions, I would request you pause and consider yourself as one of your vital assets, to provide your self-care. Are you not worth your time, cost, motivation, self-love, and energy?

'Yes, but…'

I hear your protests. Often, we will give time to other people, but we will deny loving ourselves. Would you agree? Yes? No? Maybe? Please reflect.

It's time we focus away from other people and turn to care for ourselves. Your action is not a selfish act, but the realization that our old habits are hard to change from caring for others to not caring for yourself. This journey is yours and no one else can work on healing your mind, body, and spirit. How do we start our journey?

Let's start by considering what your long-term and short-term goals are. The purpose of our long-term goals will be to recover your self-love again, dissolve your pain, promote your healing, and discover your true-life purpose, your love for other people. Our short-term goals will evolve as you spend your time reading this book, doing the different activities, talking to a supportive friend or family member, doing multiple opportunities, or writing daily in your diary.

When you read this book, each chapter will have a small introduction, activity, a sample of Kate's journal entry, and an encouragement to do a golden opportunity for loving yourself. Engaging and reading this book is difficult and anxiety may be felt.

Starting with the introduction, I will describe how to love again; otherwise, you cannot do the five strategies: 'The Crime, Slime, Grime, Time and Prime.' The description is how it applies to your love by defining the pain, recognizing the difficulties, and collecting clues about the challenges. After unfolding the strategy, an activity may be offered to write in the diary, reflect, or talk to your supportive family member or friend to find possible healing. I also suggest another option, read Kate's fictional narration.

Finally, each chapter will conclude with the offering to select one of the one hundred and fifty-six opportunities to relieve the stress and give love to our minds, bodies, and spirits. These fifty-two opportunities are offered separately for the mind, body, and spirit by loving our holistic beings.

Why do the stress relief opportunities? While studying the contents of this book, you may feel stress. Can you cope with this stress? Yes? No? Maybe? The choice is yours how to proceed through each chapter. I would request you dig deep within yourself to find the courage, to hunt for your love, to do your healing, and to experience your true-life purpose through your daily commitments.

"But, I don't have the love, courage, nor the strength, Anne."

Do I hear your self-doubt? Please understand the self-doubt may felt the first or last time. Managing our self-doubts are seen as we do something new. One method is to be bold to try a unique opportunity which will build your self-confidence.

I request you try one of the one hundred and fifty-six opportunities listed at the back of the book. The desired outcome of trying one of these golden opportunities is building your self-worth, managing your pain, and finding self-love. An example of one of these opportunities can be to walk in a beautiful setting, such as the beach or the forest.

When I practiced one of the opportunities to give myself love, I was able to continue on my challenging journey. Then, I discovered the five healing strategies which led to fruitful healing of my mind, body, and spirit, to finding my true-life purpose, to give, and to receive love. Additionally, I found Arianna Huffington's quote which she validated my findings. 'We need to accept that we won't always make the right decision, that we'll screw up royally sometimes – understanding that failure is not the opposite of success, it's part of success.' (Arianna Huffington granted for permission for this quote.)

Before we start with the first strategy, 'The Crime.' Let's remember that we are valuable and have a true-life purpose including loving self and others.

Why else are we here this very moment? The answer is we are to live a hurt free life and serve our true-life purpose. I believe that we are not to suffer from pain, but to give and receive love. What is the definition of our pain? Let's begin with chapter one known as the 'The Crime.'

The Crime

Did you know it's a crime not to heal your mind, body, and spirit? Yes, indeed, it is! How can we recover our holistic beings? By waving a magic wand is impossible to create instant healing. However, it is possible to restore our minds, bodies, and spirits using your endurance, effort, patience, courage, and self-love.

How do we proceed with our healing? Healing may begin when we cry remembering our painful memories. These recalls may be defined as those uncomfortable moments which may include:

- failing to understand what was happening;
- facing harsh life realities;
- recognizing those individuals who didn't love us;
- divorcing;
- losing a loved one to death;
- developing a chronic health problem;
- hurting from a serious car accident;

- speaking the wrong words; or
- perhaps misplacing our true-life purposes.

Being familiar with one of these stressful situations, we begin investigating our first strategy known as 'The Crime.' We understand the word crime may sound a bit harsh. Both a painful life circumstance and crime, are often defined as not premeditated, unsolved to what happens, suffered a loss, and even maybe death has occurred.

Understanding how a detective investigates a crime, we will also scrutinize our deep pain. Using similar investigative skills, we will examine our crime scene by defining our painful life event.

How do we define our crime, our past painful life situation? One procedure is to ask six questions: who, what, when, how, where, and why. These six questions will be used in our methods known as defining, recognizing, and collecting clues about the crime, the pain.

Let's start our investigation by understanding the definition of our pain. Our descriptions may include one of the following situations:

- Had a loss of a loved one by their death.
- Injured in an accident such as a car, plane, or train.
- Developed of a health problem.
- Moved to a new location.
- Had work challenges.
- Divorced.
- Had a miscarriage.
- Betrayed by a close friend, spouse, or a family member.
- Struggled with yet other traumatic situations.

After defining which situation was our pain, the raw recognition is complicated even to say what happened. Oh, my! This painful admission recognizes what our horrible situation was. Do you acknowledge your anxiety after defining your pain? Yes? No? Maybe?

Let's calm our anxiety by doing some deep breathing exercises. Please take a deep inhale, exhale, and repeat which will relax your body, center your mind, and rekindle your spirit.

Oh, what did you just say?

Your response was, 'Breathing is not helping me, Anne. It's a waste of my time!'

I disagree that breathing is not a waste of time. Let me give you an example. Ready?

Let's try a simple, deep breath while picking up your pen, looking at it, and exhale.

Please take another breath in, breathe out slowly, and notice how your breathing feels.

Please put the pen down on your desk.

Now without thinking about the pen, please take in a deep breath, and exhale.

Take another breath in and breathe out slowly.

Now, compare the two breathing exercises.

You may find that your breathing was deeper when you didn't think about your pen. Yes? Why?

Breathing is a natural relaxer for your mind, body, and spirit. The reason is your consciousness cannot focus on the pen and take an adequate breath at the same time. Your body may only take a shallow inhalation as your mind is trying to figure out what you are looking at, the pen; therefore, I would recommend exclusively focus on your breathing only.

Let's now take some deeper inhales and exhales.

Can you feel the difference in your breathing and your anxiety? Maybe? Yes? No?

Another suggestion is to read the toolkit chapter entitled 'Relaxing Breathing Exercises' or continue reading this chapter. The choice is yours.

Welcome back! We can travel this journey together. Please realize you are not alone.

Do you still feel a bit anxious now? Let's take a couple deeper, slower breaths. I'll continue when you have completed your breathing, and then we will proceed.

After defining your pain, you may have recognized that it was stressful and your life changed which affected your mind, body, and spirit. How does stress affect you?

At this moment, it is not essential to do

anything while we examine the three clues about how stress may affect our minds, bodies, and spirits. Shall we continue? Yes? No? It is acceptable to take a break if you desire. I'll be here when you return to this page.

Let's examine your discomfort affecting your body. How do you feel at this moment? Do you have pain, nausea, shortness of breath, or another physical symptom? Please stop and reflect by writing in your diary.

One response is that you couldn't understand what happened, feeling a sense of dread, or manage any number of bodily reactions such as nausea, pain, sweating, rapid heart rate, or difficulty with breathing. How do you describe your physical reactions? I would encourage you to write your observations in your journal which we will manage our negativity later.

Now let's evaluate our spirits. What is affecting your soul? Are you feeling sad, guilt, resentment, or another negative emotion?

Please take a moment to feel your spirit and then write your observations in your journal.

Our spirits may be disconnected from our feelings; then we feel separated from our core beings. Other emotions may include feeling empty, anger, sadness, guilt, frustration, or different negative responses. We will explore these negative comebacks in the two future chapters entitled 'The Slime' to manage our anger, and 'The Grime' to change our negative responses to positive emotions.

Shall we ponder what your mind is considering? Your thoughts may include: 'I don't want to think' or 'I don't even know why I am reading this book.' Yes? No? Maybe? Please take a few minutes to figure out, reflect, and journal your thoughts. When you finish, I invite you to return.

By collecting and observing these simple explanations, we recognize our anxiety about our painful situation. To decrease our pain, we must gather clues about what happened during our painful event. An effective method is journaling which may open your understanding of your pain, how your stress affected your life, and your future true-life purpose.

Did I hear your doubts? Did you say, 'Why in the world do I need to write down my feelings, thoughts, and bodily responses, Anne?'

Journaling will improve our minds, bodies, and spirits by the following benefits:

- Releasing negativity will be seen as you write each day. Our minds will not continue to write about your negativity. Slowly you will change your unwanted thoughts because you'll want positive ones.
- Developing an understanding of your current thoughts, feelings, and fears.
- Decreasing your stress is seen as you dump it into your journal.
- Increasing your self-esteem because you'll start seeing your self-value.
- Defining your relationships and their meanings in your life.

- Preserving your life passions as you describe them.
- Understanding where you used to be, where you are now, and where you will be.

For additional information about writing in your diary, please refer to the Toolkit for 'Tips About Successful Journaling.'

My dear reader, please reflect on how a detective processes a crime scene. She records her observations of the crime scene in her criminal file. Often written, criminal reports are used for lawsuits, but more important, they may record observations, interviews, photos, etc. The sleuth will review the written documentation to piece together what happened at the crime scene.

So, shall we continue by investigating our painful recollections by writing them? I hear your further protests to write in your journals. Please know writing our feelings, fears, and frustrations are one of the ways to provide our self-care merely to recognize that they exist.

Yes, I struggled with my daily writing. Sometimes I could write for only a minute while other times I wrote for over an hour. When I couldn't write, I found a creative method to express my pain by creating my imaginary character, Kate. Often, she described my thoughts, feelings, and bodily responses when I couldn't. Please do not be surprised if you struggle writing your responses. You may do the first activity listed below, read Kate's journal, or do one of the opportunities to decrease your stress. An example of a body opportunity is to sit in a warm bubble bath, listen to soft music, and allow your body to relax. Please realize that it is acceptable that you can't write in your journal.

The choice is entirely yours. When you finished your chosen activity, please join me. I will continue after Kate's diary which is enclosed in the box below.

Activity #1

What is a simple description of your pain?

Who?

What?

When"

Why?

Where?

How?

What did you discover about your pain?

Kate's Journal: The Writing

The time was 5:03 AM. I begged her for more sleep. "Please go back to sleep, Kate," I told her sternly.

I gave a belly laugh.

Kate refused as she pointed to my pen and paper, which slid to the bedroom floor the night before.

"Please pick up your pen and write my story, Anne," she begged.

I laughed and said, "No, first of all, I need

my coffee!" *I can't write my words. What the hay –
I'm now talking to my own subconscious! This is too
funny!*

Quietly, I arose out of my warm and
comfortable bed, eliminated my bodily wastes,
showered, dressed, and headed to the kitchen.

"Can we talk now?" Kate whispered as she
sat down on one of the kitchen counter chairs.

*I don't know if I could write anything
worth writing. Really? I will delay my writing. Yes,
indeed!*

"Not yet," I replied. "I need my morning
coffee, as if you don't drink it!"

I walked over to the cabinet, opened it, and
reached for the coffee grounds, filling the coffee urn
with water, and coffee grounds.

"Aren't you ready yet?" Kate demanded
impatiently as she pointed to the pen and journal.
They had magically appeared upon the kitchen table.

"Nope! Not yet," I replied as I took out a
raw egg, an English muffin, a jar of strawberry jam,
an orange, and milk from the refrigerator as I saw
Kate sat at the kitchen counter, watching my every

move. I turned on the stove burner, inserted the English muffin into the toaster, broke the egg onto the skillet, and picked up my flipper.

Pointing my egg flipper at her heart, I declared, "Not yet. I *am* a starving writer." *I have my hospital job as a registered nurse. Why do I dream about writing? What do I write about – don't want to go into those painful memories...nope!*

Kate nodded, as I continued, "You know that old saying."

"Yeah, I do."

"And I need my energy, since you, Kate, won't let me sleep, drink my coffee, or eat my breakfast! The saying is 'silence is golden.'"

"But – "

"Kate, please leave me alone for a few minutes. Okay?"

"No…. I must tell my story!" Kate demanded as she readjusted herself in the hard, wooden counter chair.

Why bother to write, but I like to tell a story.... ahh...

"In a few minutes, you shall indeed," I answered as I turned to flip my egg on the skillet, removed my English muffin from the toaster, and spread a teaspoon of strawberry jam upon my muffin. Then I peeled my orange, poured coffee, and added milk into my favorite black mug.

Appropriately thirty-five minutes later, I saw Kate sitting straight, like an angry cat. She glared at me as I finished my breakfast, sipped my coffee, and listened with my heart to my relaxing, guided music. I sat upon my separate kitchen counter chair for some chosen quiet minutes.

Upon completion of energizing my heart, body, and soul, I cleaned up after my meal. Then, I looked at my alter ego. "Yes, it is now time to begin writing about your life story, filled with multiple difficulties."

I paused before continuing, "Kate, where are you? Do tell your story, Kate. My right hand is ready. I *am* holding the pen, and waiting to write with a deep, life-filled passion."

Her valuable words flew across the page and then filled each line until I declared that I needed a break after two hours of writing! As I looked over at the kitchen counter, Kate had fallen asleep.

Welcome back! Did you define and recognize your pain? Did you collect any clues about your painful situation? Or maybe you did not even address the pain. I didn't! I'm not one bit surprised that you considered something unrelated to your pain. Are you?

What did I hear you say?

'Oh, Anne, where are we going now?'

I'm laughing. Can you laugh, too?

Oh, do I hear you ask, 'What's so funny?' The humor is seen as we, you and me, thought this healing process would be natural and done quickly. The opposite is the *darn* truth that we will need to work long and hard.

Are you puzzled while holding this book as it appears to be simple and yet so difficult? Yes, it is, and we are here together in spirit to emotionally crawl, walk, run, and even fall while going down our healing paths.

You may have another painful life event that pops up; it requests your definition and your recognition. My personal two examples may provide a powerful insight. My first example was my divorce which I felt my heart and soul were damaged beyond repair. While I was working on my healing, I soon realized the death of my dear father, my second example, was also my unreal, unfathomable pain. Neither situation was any less than the other; both events deeply wounded my heart and my deep, inner soul as well as stressed my body. I realized that I had a deep heartache. Can you relate two events in your life? Please reflect for a bit of endless time if you have another aching situation.

I questioned how I could bare the pain from these two traumatic events and yet heal them? I wandered around many a day to figure out what should I do next. My answer was to dig deeper and deeper into what I labeled as my nasty emotion, anger. I soon realized that my passion was harbored inside and had the potential to harm my body physically. As a registered nurse, I recognized some of the physically adverse health issues which may include, but are not limited to high blood pressure, hives, stomach ulcers, migraine headaches, skin lesions, and cancer.

I didn't want to face my fury, but I didn't want any physical illnesses or injuries. Ouch, that was a rotten admission that I knew that I had to manage my anger in both situations. I considered my choices and decided that I was a strong woman who lives by the saying, 'take the bull by its horns.' I knew this declaration would be that this strategy was not one moment, but extensive time to explore my pain.

Realizing I would take my time to understand my pain, I needed a minute or more to comprehend what happened to me just like you will. Please take your time to explore deeper into your pain by answering the six detective questions: who, what, where, when, how, and why. Your exploration will lead to discovering soon or later that you have anger. I did.

Before going to the next chapter, I endorse that you do one of the opportunities for your mind, body, and spirit. Please take advantage of the one hundred and fifty-six opportunities to decrease your stress.

Did I hear that your reply was, 'No!'

Why? I strongly encourage you to provide some self-care and love yourself. I can't imagine you want to hold on to the negativity which may affect your mind, body, and spirit adversely. Additionally, I would like you to realize that you will review the painful situation more than one time. Sometimes, you will be unable to face it and may turn it into an addiction such as overeating. Slowly, the reality will calm down and you can go to another strategy. One example is wanting to manage the anger which we will proceed to in the next chapter, 'The Slime.' Please realize it will not be comfortable when we take a hard look at our anger. Thank you.

The Slime

Turning our attention to our anger, we define it may be 'slimy' causing adverse effects on our bodies, minds, and spirits. Affecting our bodies, some results may include physical symptoms such as headaches, clenched fists, grinding teeth, chest pain, nausea, aches, and pains. These physical symptoms may lead to damages of various organs in our bodies such as the liver, lung, brain, skin, heart, kidneys, and immune system. In comparison, our minds may be affected by anxiety, depression, and death, whereas, our spirits may be filled with sadness, grief, guilt, fears, worries, and frustrations. When you and I define these symptoms, they affect our souls by turning into fury or resentment leading us to a more in-depth pain.

Do you recognize your anger boiling when your mind drifts to consider your painful situation? Please take a few minutes to describe your current emotion and write about it in your diary.

Did you feel anxious, fear, frustration, and maybe anger? Yes? No? Maybe? Please reflect.

Your defined, negative emotion is anger. You may experience other negative emotions which are not our focus at this moment. The other negative emotions may include sadness, grief, anxiety, worries, resentment, guilt, etc. Please note our future investigation will focus on the different negative feelings in the next chapter known as 'The Grime.' Our current strategy is to define our anger.

Studying this nasty, ugly emotion known as our anger, we will choose to achieve our long-term goal, our healing. Let's feel deeper into our passion. Our responses may be that our hurt and annoyance which may demand not to be healed. I believe you want to improve your mind, body, and spirit since you are reading this book. Please continue reading. Thank you.

For this reason, we have defined and recognized our anger. The definition of anger may also be a response to an offense and to fear our pain. Our recognition may acknowledge the depth of our anger which grew during and after our painful life situation. Do you feel the intensity of your rage?

You may shy away from looking at your anger. Our investigation will not be straightforward but will be as tough as peeling an onion. An example is seen as I'm writing this manuscript. I found my thoughts drifting to the birth of my niece's son and my desire to be a mother. My tears flowed while remembering the focus of my anger, and my recognition was when my ex-husband refused to do a sperm count and to begin understanding why I was not pregnant.

My ex-husband would not discuss why he declined a sperm count. I was furious and turned to overeat foods for comfort. This morning tears are running down my cheeks as I remember that last moment, and I realize that I need to manage my unresolved anger!

What was the trigger of your anger? Please pause to reflect. Are you feeling pissed?

Before we continue, we need to calm our anger because it will not be beneficial in our healing journey. I admit that I need to quiet my fury. Shall we take a deep breath and exhale? Yes, please take another inhale and exhale. Thank you.

Let's recognize that we are upset. Yes, we both know this procedure will be followed by the collection of our clues related to our anger. Even as I write this chapter, I'm gaining an understanding of my anger. I, too, need to investigate as we proceed. Why do I admit this? It's proof that the healing journey is an ongoing process. Do you agree?

Our investigation reveals that we are taking significant risks which removes us from our comfort zones. Leaving our safe, hidden places appear to be awful as if I'm asking you to jump off the mountaintop without a safety harness. I'm sure that you aren't feeling safe.

Each step down our paths leads to healing our minds, bodies, and spirits; discovering our true-life purpose, and finding love. Yes, I'm repeating myself, but I know you may need a positive re-enforcement. Our mutual goal is to continue collecting our clues about our anger. Our desire may be an intense, offensive emotion, motivating us to do our investigation.

Previously, we defined and recognized our nasty emotion, our anger. Your choice is whether you continue writing about your anger in the second activity. Your successful description will let you know your truth and no one else has this information. Yes, this writing may be hard, but we must do this activity to have a clearer understanding.

If you choose not to write, please read Kate's diary, or enjoy one of the mindful, spiritual, and physical opportunities. I request you try one of the one hundred and fifty-six opportunities listed at the back of the book. The desired outcome of trying one of these opportunities is building your self-worth, managing your pain, and find your self-love. An example of one of these opportunities can be to spoil yourself by going out for a meal with a friend or a family member to reconnect in their love for you. When you finish your chosen task, please join me at the end of Kate's diary.

Activity #2

Write your definition and recognition of your

anger by collecting your clues answering the six questions:

Who?

When?

Where?

What?

How?

Why?

Kate's Journal: The Onion Peel

Suddenly, I heard the back door open. My husband is home!

"Welcome home, Sean," I called out as I heard the door close. I knew it was him! I'm so blessed to have such a loving man. And to think that I got married only two months ago...

I didn't hear any response from him. My ears vibrated from the refrigerator's noisy motor and I could hear the kitchen clock tick loudly. I didn't hear even one word from him.

"How was your day?" I asked as he walked to the bathroom with his head drooped towards the carpet. My stomach flipped. "Is something wrong, Sean?" He's never this quiet! Why is he acting so strange? Sean entered the bathroom. I heard the water splashing in the bathroom sink, the water faucet is shut off and the towel rubbing against the metal rack. My stomach flopped like a hot pancake on a greased skillet as Sean broke the silence.

"Is supper ready?" he whispered as he walked into the kitchen.

"Yes. Why are you whispering?" I asked, anxiously. I flipped open my compact, applied my pink lipstick and scanned my white- chocolate colored hair. Two tears were rolling down from my dilated blue eyes, hidden behind my brown-framed glasses. Why is he acting like this? Did I do something wrong? I pulled out a corner of my blue blouse to wipe my glasses.

I returned the compact and lipstick to my

pocket, tucked my blouse into my jeans and walked to the stove as Sean wandered to the kitchen window. What does he see out there? I looked out the same window searching the western horizon, where I saw the sinking sun and heard the rumbling of distant thunder. I observed dark clouds looming over the naked maple trees and the slightly snow-covered tree branches above my rose garden. Then, I turned back to the stove, uncovered the beef stew, stirred it, reached for the yellow bowl from the kitchen cabinet and spooned the beef stew into the bowl. I picked out a small onion skin and promptly ate it. I need to stop this nervous habit of gobbling food when I'm anxious! I'll end up gaining weight, stuffing down my feelings, fears, and frustrations! ... And extra weight from overeating isn't going to protect me from anything.

I heard Sean open the refrigerator and ask in a louder voice, "do we have brownies again?" He walked over to the coffee pot, poured coffee into his mug and pushed five buttons on the microwave as he placed his mug inside.

"Yes," I replied. Someone's had a bad day! I

felt my heart racing like a doe running in the woods away from a hunter.

Within a minute, the microwave beeped, and he pulled out his coffee mug. Sean sat down at the kitchen table, poured milk into his coffee and reached for one of the biscuits. He slowly tore it apart as it fell to his plate. The sound of the biscuit hitting the china plate seemed unusually loud.

As I sat down, I noticed that Sean was rubbing his right index finger around the top of his coffee mug. Why is he rubbing his coffee mug? He usually does that when he's upset. What could he be upset about? I looked at him, searching for his eyes. He poured a spoonful of the beef stew over his biscuit.

We sat a few minutes in silence, as we began to eat our beef stew and biscuits.

Suddenly, Sean yelled. "Damn it, woman! Onions are to be skinned!"

I looked at him as my heart rate increased and I felt another sweat bead roll down my back. "Look at this onion – it's not skinned!" he boomed, showing me an onion skin in his right hand.

I watched the onion skin as he dropped it on to the table. His white knuckles swung towards my face, barely missing my mouth. I trembled like an autumn leaf in the harsh winter wind. What is happening? "What's wrong with the onion, Sean?"

"Kate, what is wrong with you?" he shouted.

I stared at him and then at the onion skin that he'd thrown onto the tablecloth.

"Damn it! I don't have to eat this slop!" he yelled as he scooped out a handful of beef stew with his bare right hand. Then, as if in slow motion, I saw the handful of beef stew flying towards me, missing my face by inches.

"Oh, my God!" I cried out. I heard his kitchen chair scrape across the floor. In seconds, he was out the back door. The door slammed, his car started and he beeped his horn loudly. What was that? My goodness, he's insane! I sat on my chair swaying like a wobbly rock on a cliff's edge.

Within minutes, the back door opened again. "Are you coming, woman?" he yelled.

"No," I said as my heart began beating faster.

"You will come now! Do you hear me?" he

fumed.

I gripped my chair as I watched Sean charging around the kitchen like a raging bull. I caught his eyes; they were bloodshot. I stood up, grabbed my purse and jacket from the clothing rack. I better do what he says. I've never seen him like this before. I felt him staring at me behind me as I cautiously turned around and then he was gone. Another sweat bead flowed down my back. I heard him slam the back door, so I promptly followed him to the car.

We drove to the local restaurant, racing dangerously down the road. God help me! Please don't let us get into an accident.

Uncomfortable and frozen with his erratic driving, I sat there trembling as he passed several cars, cutting them off. I felt nauseated as my body swung back and forward, in sync with his swerving in between cars. Then in an unrecognizable stranger's voice, he ranted, "You know you could have done better, but you always do things half-assed. Why are you like that?"

I stared at him and felt my bowels start to

spasm. He raged, "If I can't have you, no man will! You'll never leave me alive if you cheat on me!" Sean pounded violently on the steering wheel with his fists as he repeated these words, "You'll never leave me alive if you cheat on me..." I felt frozen.

Finally, we arrived at the restaurant and were seated by the hostess. The waitress took Sean's order. Mine was a cup of coffee and skim milk. During the meal, we both sat there in silence as he ate his meal. I stirred and sipped my coffee, which tasted unusually bitter.

There was only silence.

When he finished his meal, we left the restaurant. I suddenly felt my bowels cramping on the ride home. I screamed at my husband, "Sean, I need the bathroom! Please stop at the next gas station!"

"Kate, you can wait until we get home to go to the bathroom," he retorted.

"No, I need to go now!" I shifted my behind, as a jumping potato does on a hot frying pan. I stared out the car window, looking in the side mirror, watching the gas station behind us that he had passed.

"Damn it, Kate. We're almost home. Hold it!"

he exclaimed, aggressively.

"Please, Sean. There is a restaurant down the street. I need the bathroom now!"

Sean passed three more cars, cutting them off by inches. God, please get us home safely. I'm so scared! "Please, Sean – I need the bathroom." I can't understand why he doesn't hear me. I need the bathroom, and he's ignoring me!

"Damn it, Kate – hold it!" he yelled again.

"I can't!" I cried as a sharp cramp stabbed my lower stomach. "Please, Sean. I'm going to have diarrhea all over this car seat!"

Suddenly, Sean put on the turn signal and made a sharp right-hand turn into a restaurant parking lot. I jerked forward as he slammed on the brakes. Finally! Quickly fumbling to open the car door, I wiped my sweaty hands on my pants for the third time.

"Damn it! Open the damn door, bitch!" he bellowed.

I ignored him and jolted the car door open. What the heck is wrong with him today? What did I do? At last, I ran into the restaurant, sped past the other customers, flung open the bathroom door, unzipped my pants, and barely managed to sit down when my bowels released explosive diarrhea. Holy crap! Literally! What is going on? I can't believe this is happening. What did I do wrong? God, it must be my nerves why else would I have diarrhea?

After my emergency bathroom trip, I returned to the car. We didn't say one word the rest of the journey home. As I entered the house, I focused my attention on placing the remaining beef stew into the refrigerator and cleaning up the kitchen. When I was done, I sat at my writing desk and began to write: 'Whatever happened to the romantic, loving man I married?

When we wrote another definition of our anger, we soon recognized some heavy stuff. Yes, let's use the word stuff because you will have a different understanding of your passion. What are we acknowledging? Hmmm...

Oh, you may brashly say, 'Let's not go there anymore, Anne!'

Yes, my dear reader, we are going there. When I wrote about the onion situation, my heart was racing and feeling my anger. I had to take time to calm myself because I didn't want to face my wrath. Do you sense your rage?

Or do I hear you screaming, 'No! I'm not dealing with this shit now?'

Yes, I hear you don't want to define and recognize your anger arising from your painful situation. I would recommend continuing our healing journey.

How? Calm yourself down, my dear reader. I am. Maybe we may take some deep breaths. Please take a deep inhale and exhale perhaps another one. I'm still here with you. I'm doing my breathing.

Yes, I may be not in a physical being with you. However, I feel your spirit as I write these words knowing this threatening experience as our anger. Please understand that your experience may be challenging to face the harsh reality of defining, recognizing it, and collecting clues.

Yes, you may want to go back into the safe space, but it is fruitless. To quit working on your healing will have no value in your discovery of your love and precious, future true-life purpose. Right? Please pause and reflect.

Let's now get real about our true anger. My anger was why in the **hell** did I marry my ex-husband? He was such a royal pain in the ass. I wanted to have children, and he didn't give me that opportunity. I also recognize my other fury was why did Dad die? Oh, I wrote my truth, and it is making me feel insecure; however, I found freedom on many pages in my multiple journals.

Are you ready to read your writing about your truth or do you want to read Kate's journal? I realized that I just wrote mine. Does your diary reflect your anger? Yes? No? Maybe? The choice is entirely and undeniably your choice. I will continue at the end of Kate's next journal entry about her anger.

Kate's Journal: Anger

I am so angry when I remember when I came back from a nursing conference. My husband was such an ass!

I heard every one of my steps as the ice-covered snow crunched under my feet, echoing in the starless night. My heart rate quickened, and my breathing got shallower as I made it to the back doorstep. *Calm down, Kate Louise. You have nothing to fear but fear itself.*

I opened the back door to an eerily quiet house. The kitchen clock read 2:05 AM. I quickly removed my boots and slipped on my wool slippers. I laid my purse down quietly on the hallway table and removed my hat, scarf, and gloves. On my way down the hallway, the television from the master bedroom television was blaring. 'The neighbor reported that his owner was beating the German Shepherd dog; he reported it to the authorities. The dog is being taken to the local animal shelter…,' I heard the female television announcer say. *Oh God, I hope this doesn't give Sean any ideas to beat me, too. I should've called him.* I tiptoed past the master bedroom door into the bathroom, and heard, "Kate?"

My voice sounded squeaky and fearful, like a trapped mouse. "Yes?" I answered, hesitantly.

In an instant, Sean was standing at the bedroom door, butt naked. He looked at me blankly and slipped into my floral bathrobe. I looked up at him, trying to determine what kind of mood he was in.

After a short pause, he walked past me and into the kitchen. I followed him from afar, fearfully anticipating what would come next. He turned on the kitchen overhead light and turned off the stove light. *What is going on? He always leaves the stove light on. I know it stresses him out when it's off! Why is he acting so oddly? He has never done this before!*

"How was he?" Sean said, locking his dark black eyes with mine. I could sense the anger inside of him; I took a deep breath. *How was who? Please, don't tell me he thinks I'm cheating!*

Frustrated, I placed my right hand in my jeans pocket and started crumpling my luggage tags in my hand.

"Are those his luggage tags?" Sean asked, grabbing them from my hand.

What the hell?! I've had enough of this bullshit! He always thinks I'm lying. I'm sick of this! "No! Damn it, Sean." I yelled. I snatched the tags back from him, ran to the bathroom, ripped the tags into pieces, and promptly flushed them down the toilet. *Why is he accusing me of cheating on him? He must be cheating on me if he is accusing me! Isn't that how it works? You accuse other people of things you are guilty of? This must mean Sean cheated on me with another woman or man. I have never cheated on him! I'm done with this marriage! It's over!*

I was relieved that Sean hadn't followed me into the bathroom. *Shit – does that make me look guilty now that I've flushed those tags down the toilet? What if he beats me now that I ran off with them?* I returned to the kitchen with a lump in my stomach. Sean was rinsing out the coffee pot, took out a coffee filter, and coffee grounds from the cupboard reached for a spoon from the silverware drawer and poured the coffee grounds into the filter. *Why is he having coffee at 2 AM? He seems jittery enough to me already!*

"Well, how was he?" he demanded.

Wow, Sean. Do you want to continue with this, huh?

What's next? Are you going to accuse me of having sex with another man? "Who are you talking about?" I asked, sarcastically, with more self-confidence this time.

"The man you met on the Internet."

The man I met on the Internet. Unbelievable! Maybe it's you, Sean, who met a man on the Internet! "I did not comply with any man. I attended a nursing conference," I stated matter-of-factly.

"The hell you did!" he yelled, slamming his coffee mug on the kitchen table.

"Yes, I did," I said, trying to keep my voice steady. I reached for the mail on the kitchen table, but before I could pick it up, he extended his hand, and pushed the letter onto the floor.

"Pick the mail up now, bitch," he screamed.

What the fuck is his problem? He's acting like

a giant asshole! I looked at him in disbelief. If I don't pick up the mail, he's gonna get violent. I stooped down to gather the mail. This marriage is done! I am fed up of this nonsense!

Sean continued, "I went to the hospital while you were gone and no one knew where you were. I called your mother, sister, and brothers. No one knew your whereabouts. Who was he? Whose luggage tags were those?"

Well, I didn't tell Mom, Claire, my brothers or friends where I was. So, naturally, no one would know and wouldn't have to lie to me! Asshole! "One of the girls from our group got sick and vomited at the airport check-in on the way back to Albany. We helped her clean up. I forgot to give her tags back." I was so terrified that Sean would hit me that I didn't even know what I was saying anymore. In trying to lie to him about the tags, I had messed up my cover-up about the nursing conference. *Oh, my God! What the heck did I just do? I can't believe I told him I was at the airport! He thought I had driven to this 'conference'! He's gonna flip!*

"That is a lie! Who was he?" he boomed. His face was bright red.

"Sean, what are you talking about?" I answered. Why couldn't I keep my stupid mouth shut about the airport! Of course, he doesn't believe me now!

"You're cheating on me, and you're fucking up our marriage!" he yelled.

"You're a damn fool. I never cheated on you, not even for a single minute!" I shouted back at him, without thinking. Adrenalin was pumping hard through my veins, and I mustered up the unbelievable courage to say, "Our marriage is over!" *Am I crazy? He's going to kill me!*

"What the hell are you talking about?" Sean screamed, violently throwing his kitchen chair to the floor.

"I never cheated on you! You insist on believing that I did! Our marriage is over because you have cheated on me!" I shouted. *Where is all this confidence coming from?*

"Oh yeah? What are you gonna do now? You don't have it in you to leave me!" Sean boomed again in a threatening voice, slowly stepping towards me. His hands were balled up into massive fists.

"Watch me!" I screamed, defiantly. I could feel my hands trembling and clenched them by my side.

"What are you saying? You won't leave me!" his voice was much lower now; his tone was almost unrecognizable.

"Watch me!" I repeated sternly, daringly looking straight into his black eyes. "You think I'm not fair or something? My God! How do you have the nerve to say that I cheated?"

Sean slumped his shoulders, broke eye contact and shied away from my direct glare.

"And what have I done to you?" he asked. His sudden weak posture gave me more courage to continue my outburst.

"Lies! You lied to me, Sean! The foundation of our marriage is based on a lie! The cruelest lie that you kept from me is the most painful one. You never revealed the truth." The words came out of my mouth before I even realize what I was implying. *Of course!*

Sean must be gay. It would be a logical explanation to his disappearances late at night, to the fact that we rarely have sex... I took a deep breath and pointed to the floral bathrobe he was wearing. "Because you know the truth that you have kept from me. I trusted and believed in you. I can't believe anything else you say."

Sean unclenched his fists and stood there without saying one word.

I turned away from him, stomped into the hallway and dropped the mail on the hallway table. "I am going to bed!" I exclaimed. I walked into the master bedroom and slammed the door.

I pulled out my white nightgown from the dresser drawer and began to undress. Sean opened the door and stood there for a few minutes as the television blared. *Did my boldness mean that I was in for a beating?* I continued to change into my nightgown, tensely anticipating what would happen next.

What did you discover? My discovery was to describe my thoughts or emotions by using my five senses. How? I realized that my senses might lead to understanding my anger and my painful situation. Do you want to explore your experience by using the five senses? Please consider doing the third activity.

Activity #3

Please write about either your pain or your anger. Then, analyze your five senses as to the following:

1. What was your feeling?

2. What do you smell?

3. What do you taste?

4. What do you hear?

5. What do you see?

6. Do these senses make you want to cry?

7. Please allow your tears to flow.

8. Take a deep breath and exhale.

9. Try a distraction or do one of the opportunities to heal your mind, body, or spirit.

10. When you completed an opportunity, did you want to write about how to survive while experiencing your anger?

We can experience our five senses: smell, hearing, touch, taste, and sight related to understanding our pain. The real freedom was to appreciate my honesty to myself as to what was my anger. How did I achieve this honesty? Let's explore the five senses.

Pull out your diary, read your entry related to the first sense, smell. How did you describe your sense known as smell? Maybe you did not write a description. Do you want to reconsider journaling now about what you smelled during your painful situation? Yes? No? Again, it is your choice.

What does your journal reflect what you saw during your painful experience? Can you remember a past location? What did you observe with the other person? If you don't read your visual description, do you want to take this moment to describe it now?

Can you feel the clothes you wore that day? Do you feel sweaty, hot, chilled, or cold? Or perhaps you feel your physical body hurts? You are safe now and can explore this situation. Or maybe you are not ready. The choice is yours to either read or write a description.

Please consider what you taste. Do you remember any foods or drinks related to your painful situation? Are you at home, out at a restaurant, picnic, party, coffee café, or any other site? Is it time to read or write about what you tasted during the uncomfortable event?

Finally, let's turn our attention to your hearing. What do you hear? Listen to the other person's words. What did you perceive in the exchange of words or lack of them? What did you reply? Did you read or want to write a description of what you heard?

Often when our painful situation occurred, we may have denied our nasty, horrible outrage, but our senses record answers to our mental, physical, and spiritual responses. Some of our responses may be not to feel our anger or to discuss what was happening. Our journal entries may reflect a wide range of emotions similar to Elizabeth Kubler-Ross's death and dying theory. She wrote about the feelings ranging from denial, anger, depression, bargaining, and acceptance.

Did you write about one of these feelings in your diary? I'm confident that you may have one emotion or another one not listed. So, what is the meaning of our negative emotions?

Initially, I denied that my negativity. I'm quite sure that you may have also done the same. Is there more than anger? Wanting to understand my anger, I read many research articles. One article was written by Ms. Kim Pratt as found on the website,

https://healthypsych.com/psychology-tools-what-is-anger-a-secondary-emotion/ She explained that anger is a secondary emotion that covers primary emotions which may include fear, frustration, guilt, shame, resentment, doubt, sadness, and countless other less than positive responses. She suggested recognizing having anger and what it covers. Then, she suggests managing our anger and our other negative emotions. Let's proceed to the next chapter, 'The Grime,' for the intention to manage our anger and other negative emotions.

The Grime

Negative feelings permit us to become the perfect victims, and then we don't want to heal our minds, bodies, and spirits. It is normal to feel our negativity when our life expectations are not met. Then, we won't let our non-positive emotions fade. However, you and I have chosen to be on this healing strategy, 'The Grime,' together and want to continue to manage our anger and our other negative emotions.

Why do I label this strategy, grime? Please reflect when you are doing some serious cleaning in your home such as cleaning a bathtub or shower stall that it is not easy. In comparison, feeling these negative emotions are similar to hard cleaning off the grime in the bathtub and shower stall. Once you see the grime removed from the bathroom, you feel pleased, and so shall we feel happier when we clean the filth form of our anger and negative emotions.

When we become aware of our anger, we identify that it is a cover for other negative emotions. What are our other negative emotions? They may be defined as fear, frustration, guilt, shame, resentment, doubt, sadness, and countless other less than positive responses.

When we reflect on our painful situation, please pause and pull out our journals. Write about your rage by digging deeper into the definition and also the recognition of the grimy passion underneath. This action is to consider our fourth activity. Are you ready?

Activity #4

1. How do you feel? Let's examine our bodies by:

    a. Close your eyes

    b. Feel your body's sensations – do you have chest tightness, a knot in your stomach, a headache, or a feeling of fatigue?

2. Don't evaluate your feelings just feel them.

While you are feeling your mind, body, and spirit for the negative emotions, we soon recognize we may be experiencing sadness, frustration, fear, anxiety, and the list continues. To change these negative emotions to positive ones, we may feel and listen to our inner self-talk for our goal, to heal our mind, body, and spirit.

Activity #5

1. How do you express this anger or negative emotion?
2. How do you respond to a negative emotion?
3. Do you overeat, shop, have sex, do drugs, or another method?
4. Describe your answers in your journal.

Shall we do another activity of feeling your emotion? Please take a moment to continue writing in your journal, read Kate's journal, or join me after Kate's diary entry about not dealing with her negative emotions, but she was eating ice cream instead.

Kate's Journal: Ice Cream Vs Anger

Suddenly, Sean came out from behind me. I stared at him in disbelief. He was wearing my floral bathrobe! What the hell? Shit! ... I hope he didn't hear my conversation about him! His massive torso and flabby arms protruded from my robe, and I gazed upon his broad shoulders and gigantic hands. My God! Those hands look like they could be used as weapons!

"Why are you talking to your mother about our business?" Sean shouted.

"I'm not." I shied away from him as I tiptoed backward three steps and rounded my shoulders forward.

"Damn you, Kate. It's none of her fucking business! None! Do you hear me?"

"I hear you, but…"

He cut me off mid-sentence. "Kate, you're not talking to your mother! Shut up, bitch."

I opened my mouth to speak, but then as if in

slow motion, I watched Sean forcefully grab the cordless phone. "My God, Sean..." I said under my breath. He pulled the phone off the phone base. What is happening? As if in even slower motion, I watched Sean throw the phone against the back door.

"My God, Sean! What are you doing?" I yelled.

"Shut up, bitch!"

"Sean!" I cried.

"Damnit. Shut the hell up, bitch," he blasted.

The sound was as loud as a bowling ball hitting pins. It resonated in my ears as the phone shattered into pieces onto the kitchen floor. Sean ranted, "From NOW on, you will never talk to your mother about OUR problems!" I glared at Sean as he continued, "Clean up this DAMN mess, bitch! I should have never married YOU!" He stomped aggressively towards me.

This can't be happening! No, he wouldn't dare hurt me! He's never laid a finger on me! I froze momentarily and then jumped backward to avoid him.

"Damn it, Kate! Damn you!"

He came even closer to me. You aren't going to hurt me! "Sean, what the hell are you doing?" I eyed him cautiously. I glanced at the broken phone pieces and the damaged kitchen door. What is going on? This is such a trivial happening over a lousy onion skin… "Oh, my God," I said in an unfamiliar trembling voice.

"Damn you!" He attempted to grab me. He yelled, "Do you HEAR me?"

I fretfully looked at his black eyes and his white knuckled fists as they came towards my face.

"Sean!" I screamed as his large hands reached for my face and missed it by inches. My God! Did he try to hit me? I felt more sweat pour down my face and my heart beating faster. I dived away from his threatening entrapment. Sean's not going to hurt me! He wouldn't!

Shit - I can't call Mom now – the phone is broken! What do I do? You have to calm down, Kate! I should act like nothing is happening.

Don't fuel the fire, Kate. I should clean up this mess!

I turned and walked to the closet as Sean stood with his hands on his hips, his pale face dripped with sweat beads as his chest rose and fell like a harsh wintery storm wind. His eyes looked like black darts aimed to hit my unprotected heart. He spun around and marched into the living room. I feel so humiliated! Oh, God help me. What have I done? Please forgive my sins. I ask this in Jesus' name. Amen. I can't leave this marriage. I made my wedding vows – 'until death do us part... In sickness and health'... What would Mom say? Oh goodness, I know what she would say: 'Do not cry those lousy crocodile tears! Honor your marriage vows until death!' God, where are you? I need your protection! This can't be happening to me – Is this real? I anxiously looked across the kitchen. What do I do? Damn it! I'm gonna turn to my dear old friend, ice cream. I'll push this out of my mind: Ice cream will comfort me. I know it will make me feel good. I hastily grabbed a spoon from the silverware drawer and a small plastic black bowl from the cupboard. I opened the freezer door and grabbed the mint chocolate chip ice cream.

Immediately, I opened the container, jabbed into the ice cream and scooped out a big spoonful. Without much thought, I opened my mouth and gobbled it. I returned my large spoon into the ice cream and filled the bowl without regard to the amount. Closing the container, I put it back into the freezer. I ran to the master bedroom with the ice cream and spoon in tow. Abruptly, I slammed the bedroom door shut, hearing the door vibrate behind me. I quickly ate the ice cream without enjoyment – stuffing down my negative, painful feelings.

As I focused on the ice cream, I ignored my burning question: 'Is this the first time anything occurred in my relationship that bothered me?' I brushed off the thought. I'm not going to answer that question. My priority is to eat this ice cream! I thought about Sean screaming about the onion skin, throwing the telephone and attempting to grab me. What is causing Sean to be so angry? What do I do now? Do I go to bed with him? Am I safe when he returns to bed? I wish I could stop these damn tears. I should curl up in bed and go to sleep.

What did you discover in your journaling? I ignored feeling my hurting mind, body, and spirit by eating the more ice cream. Have you overeaten? Drunk excessively? Shopped too much? Taken drugs? Any extreme action is not the solution.

Since we are emotionally starving, we'll subconsciously try to fill our void by overeating or engaging in another painful activity such as drinking alcohol, excessive shopping, or taking drugs. It's never about the excess weight or harming our physical body; it's to deny our pain or not to live our true-life purpose. You and I must not only acknowledge our painful situations but also understand our anger and negative emotions for the purpose to heal and to live our true-life purposes.

Denying our life determination, we often hurt quietly through these painful events while the passion embeds deep into our subconscious. Our trust in ourselves and other people erode if we don't process the definition or recognition of our negative feelings.

These facts hide within our subconscious which may never be understood. Our goal is to awake our subconscious and practice self-love again. When our love occurs, we look for ways to heal our minds, bodies, and spirits.

Why heal our holistic beings? The rationale for healing is to discover our painful feelings which may hide within our minds, bodies, and spirits. Don't you deserve a better life than living in negativity? You don't owe the objective of your pain, the other person or event, to control your life. How can we look more in-depth? Yes, another activity is to collect our evidence about our bodily responses.

Did I hear you say, 'What another activity?'

Yes, let's do it.

What did you say?

"Anne, that's easy for you to say. You have all the answers."

My response is no. These negative emotions and activities are ones that I have experienced even as I sat down to write this book. I'm aware that I also have more digging into my negative emotions. Are you ready? Please know that I am here to help you. So, shall we continue?

Activity #6

Please write a more profound definition and recognition of your negativity by asking the six questions:

Who?

What?

When?

Where?

How?

Why?

When I dug into my other negative emotions, I discovered how deep my fury was. Please read Kate's diary entry and feel the pain with the attempt to commit suicide.

Kate's Journal: Suicide

My alarm vibrated at 4:30 AM and I woke up abruptly. I had managed to sleep only about one hour. Today was the day! The past two months had consisted of planning my suicide to the very last detail.

The night before, I had gone over my suicide plan for the very last time: reviewing, challenging, and examining every aspect. It was set as my plan would be executed perfectly. But it was daring and called for no screw-ups.

*I will finally be free once I'm dead. I won't have to suffer over Sean. I won't have to feel worthless. I'll be able to let go of all my sorrow and misery. And if it fails…well – it just better not fails…*I slipped out of bed discretely. I knew that Sean, sleeping like an old bear, would not hear me getting out of bed.

Before leaving the room, I forced myself to give him one last look. His flabby stomach was exposed and his slightly drooling mouth was pressed open against his pillow. His snoring was loud and the smell of his sweat travelled to my nostrils. *I don't* love this man. *I certainly won't be missing him! He has been horrible to me. He deserves to live alone.*

I quickly dressed in the bathroom and decided to skip eating breakfast. As someone who always ate to appease my anxiety, this was unusual for me. I simply wasn't hungry. I didn't care anymore. Nothing mattered. *I feel hollow, so maybe my stomach should be just as empty as I feel this morning... Maybe I'll lose weight! Ha! That'll serve me well once I'm dead...* I giggled at my terribly dark sense of humor and grabbed my car keys.

Within ten minutes, I was out in the cold weather, on the snowy ramp merging onto the interstate. I drove for five miles on the empty roads when I finally saw a black truck loaded with pine logs and no other trucks or cars around. *Perfect. I can catch up to it within a couple of minutes. Then I'll ram into the back of it.* I looked at my speedometer, which read sixty miles per hour. I stepped on the gas pedal and watched my speed increase fast. *Come on, Kate, it's time.* The speedometer read sixty-five mph, then seventy mph, seventy-five mph and soon eight-five mph. The thirteen-year-old car was beginning to vibrate and rattle. I felt my heart pounding hard in my chest, my breathing got shallower and shallower. *Steady, Kate, steady. You can do this.* Beads of sweat were pouring down my spine. *God, please forgive me as I take my life I beg you to consider taking me to heaven. I am your child – don't forsake me.*

The rattling of the car was all I focused on. I was coming up to the slow truck at high speed now and would crash into the back of it with full force. *Less than a minute now... It's almost time... God, please forgive me.* I took one last deep breath and closed my eyes as a lone tear ran down my cheek.

"Stop! Don't kill yourself, Kate Louise!"

What the hell? Who said that? I swerved off the road onto the narrow shoulder lane in a panic. Terrified, I gripped the steering wheel, fighting to regain control over my rusty old red sedan coupe... I jerked my little car back onto the snow-covered highway; I began speeding down the road again to catch up to the truck. Sweat poured down my face as I tightened my hands around the steering wheel. My dark blue blouse was soaked with perspiration. *Where the heck had that voice come from? Is someone in the car?*

"Who are you?" I screamed, zooming down the dark interstate, "Who are you?" I looked in my rear-view mirror, searching the back seat to see if someone was in the car with me. The back seat was empty. *Where did that voice come from? Agitated,* I turned my head to check the front passenger seat to my right. *Am I hallucinating?* No one was there either; there was only my day- planner laying on the front seat. It was opened to Friday, April 13, 1990. I had morbidly scribbled in it earlier, marking "My Death" in the 5 AM appointment slot. *I'm alone – I'm being crazy. Keep driving, Kate. Speed back up to catch up to that semi-truck.*

"I am your angel." The loud spiritual voice echoed in the car, making me recoil instantly back in my seat. Suddenly, in the corner of my eye, a shape appeared to my right; I jerked my head back towards the passenger seat. That's when I saw him. My hands felt unsteady on the steering wheel as I stared in disbelief at the white-haired man dressed in all white. *Am I dreaming? A bright lightning bolt lit up the sky* overhead, turning the dark night into daytime in a quick flash.

The brightness lit up the blue eyes on the old man's calm face. A clap of thunder boomed so loud that my ears began to ring. *Nothing's going to foil your plan, Kate. This man can't be real.* My car shook as I began hitting the rumble strips on the road, I jerked my head back to swerve into my lane again and align my car with the road. The gloomy chilly night had instantly turned dark again and I could barely make out the maple trees blowing in the wind.

Who the hell are you? Why are you here? I screamed to the man, turning to him once more. The stranger didn't answer. I strained my eyes to make out his features in the darkness. He was sitting quietly with his hands folded into a prayer formation. A peaceful smile spreads across his wrinkled face. I yanked my head back to the empty road and glanced at my speedometer, which read ninety mph. "Who are you? **Damn you!**" I yelled.

I pressed my right foot harder on the gas pedal. I kept speeding down the murky highway into the stormy night, finally catching up to the semi-truck, surrounded by lightning flashes and claps of thunder.

In my hysteric state, thoughts raced through my mind as to the logistics and the meaning behind my premediated suicide plan. I had planned to slam into the semi-truck, loaded with huge pine logs, which would bury into my big breasts. My fat body would be crushed. I would have no chance of survival. I knew this was a foolproof way of dying; emergency medics would be unable to bring me back to the living. The state police would investigate my death. They would see my red blood oozing from my corpse in the interior of my red car.

They would quickly rule it a suicide. The innocent truck driver wouldn't get any points removed from his license. He wouldn't have to feel guilty for my death. His life would be worth living. *My life, though, is not worth living.* I thought to myself after having replayed my suicide plan in a flash. I turned to glance back at the old man, as the hail crashed down with an ear-piercing sound onto the roof and windshield. His presence was overwhelming.

He isn't real, Kate!

Focus on your suicide plan. No one is going to miss you, anyways. I'm sure my family and Sean will behave properly during my funeral; they're good at putting up a front. And anyways, the one thing that I desire from them was the one thing that was missing: their love. It's not worth living. I took a deep defeated breath, thinking about how Sean was no longer fulfilling his role as a husband. All he offered me was unpredictable spouts of anger and demeaning remarks. A wave of nausea overcame me as I thought of what I had put up with all this time. *I give up! I fucking give up!*

"I will be with you and your life *will* change!" said the man in a soft voice, interrupting my persistent thoughts.

Leave me alone! Let me take my life. I can't live any longer with these feelings of misery and rejection. **"Who are you?"** I screamed again. *Why wasn't he leaving me in peace?* Suddenly our blue eyes locked together and an instantaneous downpour of serenity flooded my frame. In a heartbeat, I felt an incredibly strong, unexpected and uncontrollable desire to slow my car down and pull over, as though I was being divinely guided. *Oh, my God! You've sent me a real angel, haven't you? This old man must be my protective angel. God must want me to live! ... But, what for?*

My change of heart was immediate and unwavering. *There must be a purpose to His plan and I cannot carry out my suicide mission with my angel here beside me! He wants me to live. I don't know why – but I must have faith that God works in mysterious ways and has a plan for me.* I found a safe spot on the side of the highway, pulled over and turned to my right to speak with my angel. He was no longer there. I quickly scanned every corner of my car, searching for him. He was gone, but the feeling of serenity he had filled me with remained deep within my heart. I watched the semi-truck disappear into the distance ahead of me.

God sent me an angel. I'm cared for. I'm loved. I can't ignore His sign. Tears rushed to my eyes as I finally realized I wasn't alone. I cried for what seemed like hours until I had no more tears left to cry.

I looked up at my face in the sun visor mirror above me. My eyes were bloodshot and my eyelids swollen. I wiped off my wet face with my cold hand.

What now?

I sat there without making a sound. The storm had finally subsided. It was as though time was on pause. After sitting motionless for what felt like at least another hour, I finally decided it was time to get my act together. *Well... no good is going to come from staying here any longer. I may as well return to the house. Maybe if I go for a walk, it'll help me figure out what I should do. That usually helps me find answers to my problems.*

After writing about our identified emotion, we dug deeper into our 'grime' to collect more clues. How do we discover more? Are you curious? I know I dug deeper due to my curiosity!

How do we dig deeper? Let's consider our detective's actions. She would collect evidence and find the motive for a crime. She would be interviewing witnesses about the wrongdoing as to what happened, who was involved, when did it occur, where did the crime occur, why did it occur, and how did the crime occur. Her goal was to solve the crime.

Isn't our similar intention to understand our pain? The detective's actions are comparable because we define, recognize, collect our information by interviewing family, friends, and co-workers, and documenting in our journal. The purpose of our recording is to understand our more profound negative emotions in the next activity.

Activity #7

1. Interview your family members, friends, co-workers, and any other individuals that are aware of your pain situation.
2. Questions may include:

    a. What happened?

    b. Who was involved?

    c. When did it occur?

d. Where did it occur?

e. Why?

f. How did it happen?

During our investigation, our negative emotions may be intense, and we can de-stress by taking a deep inhale, exhale, and more breathing if needed. I am now breathing some deeper inhales and exhales, are you? Shall we resume our investigation or is it time for a break? The choice is yours.

Identify, recognize, preserve your current emotion, and honor it. Please understand that your anger was a cover for other more profound, hidden negative feelings. Yes, we both know that we must move forward and find out more about these darker emotions. They may include sadness, depression, guilt, frustration, and the list go on.

I can hear you say, 'But Anne …this is journey should be smooth from one chapter to the next chapter. Right?'

My response is nope! It is not the 'yellow brick road.' Even as I'm writing this book, I am jumping from one strategy to the next. I have hopped from analyzing the crime to question as to what I am to figure out my next strategy. I assess that you're questioning whether to continue. Yes, please do. It is not time to throw in the towel and quit. Can you continue to stay with me a little bit longer? Yes! Great!

After all, we want to know our truth. Should we look at our recordings about those interviews with other individuals? They took an undetermined amount of time to answer all the questions to examine our crime, pain; slime, our anger; and our grime, our negative emotions.

If you are not interested in reading your journal, maybe you want to write your thoughts, do an opportunity such as a workout exercise, walk, reflect, read Kate's diary, or jump forward after Kate's writing. Again, the choice is yours!

Kate's Journal: What do I understand?

As I walked out of the house, I grabbed my trusty rope and tied it around my waist out of habit. The sun was rising. I made sure to tread quietly 0n my way down the driveway towards the woods, so as to not wake up my German Shephard, Heartthrob. *Please forgive me, Heartthrob. I need time alone to think.* I hiked up the familiar forest path beside the Swan Lake, jumping over the various outgrown bushes, and trees. I walked with the uneasy gait of a frightened child, looking out for vines, as my jacket occasionally got hooked on to them. Trees and undergrowth surrounded me; I felt the gentle early morning breeze on my face. The sweet forest odors enveloped me as the dry wood and leftover hardened snow cracked under my feet. Instead of continuing to walk down my favorite path as I had intended, I felt a renewed confidence, and decided to take an unfamiliar, unmarked path.

As I was discovering the beautiful trees, bushes, and flowers on this new path, I wasn't paying attention to my footing anymore. Suddenly, I slipped backwards and fell hard four feet down into a steep black cave. I slammed into the rock on my buttocks; my right forearm rammed into the cold side of the cave. Before I could gain any sense of orientation and balance, my body slid further into the cave and toppled downwards over a ridge. I flew through the air for a split second before slamming down hard onto stones, rocks, and plants that ripped at my clothing. I rapidly tumbled down the cave's steep slope uncontrollably until my body crashed into a muddy, rocky pool of water. I moaned in agony, lying in the freezing water as the pain crept into my every joint and bone. I held my breath in an attempt to ease the pain.

As my eyes regained their focus, I scanned my surroundings in the dimly lit cave. My backpack was lying across the pool from me. It would be useless to try to reach out for it. Under my ripped clothes, I could see my skin abrasions. I started looking around for a way out. Even if I managed to pull myself up, it would be too steep to climb out of this pool. I struggled to sit up; I was struck by dizziness. I laid back down with the cave's dim light spinning overhead; I lost consciousness.

When I awoke, the quality of the light in the cave had changed. My entire body was shaking from the cold. *How long have I been out for? My best* estimate was that it must have been about 2 PM. *I must have been out cold for hours!*

"Help! Somebody help!" My voice echoed in the cave. I called out frantically for help until my voice was hoarse. *I may as well rest my voice. No one's here. I'll bet, my husband, Sean, hasn't even realized I'm gone.* My thoughts were running through my mind at a mile a minute. I remembered Sean's first fit of rage; the onion skin incident; how he had thrown the phone, our disastrous wedding day, and our horrible dates with his friend, Jack. *I'm not going to die here. How am I supposed to move forward now that I decided to live? There is no way in hell I can stay married to Sean.* It felt as though the cold water had seeped into my very core. I began to cry hysterically until I couldn't cry another tear. *All my dreams of marriage are gone. What do I do? How do I get out of this hellhole I've gotten myself into?*

My tired eyes were drawn to a strange shape crouching on the steep slope that I had fallen down from. *What is that? Is this a person?* I sat up with a start with strength I didn't realize I still had in me.

"Look around – Kate Louise, you have the tools you need to get yourself out of your situation," said a tranquil voice.

I squinted my eyes, trying to make sense of the shape that had just spoken to me. *Am I suffering from a concussion?* My eyes finally focused in on him. I immediately recognized the man's snow-white hair and sky-blue eyes. "Who are you? Are you my angel?" I asked in a hopeful tone.

"You have the answers to your questions about how to solve your problems," he said in a reassuring, loving voice. "You can pull yourself out. I have faith in you. Now, Kate Louise, get up, and get out." He gave me a warm smile and turned his back to me.

"Don't leave me! What do I do?" I protested in a hoarse voice. In the blink of an eye, he was gone.

My hands instinctively reached for my waist, as if they were spiritually guided. I looked down and discovered the rope that I had tied around my waist before leaving the house. It had rubbed against my skin, causing it to bleed.

Out of the blue, President Franklin D. Roosevelt's saying resonated in my mind: 'When you come to the end of your rope, tie a knot and hang on.' *That's the answer!* I took my rope, tied a knot to a branch from a fallen tree that was within my reach and pulled myself up into a standing position. *I'm going to get out of this frightening cave.* I focused on the bright light beaming from the entrance of the cave. *How do I get out of here?* I stood still, trying to keep my balance. The rope was pulling at my waist.

Wait a minute! The answer is right in front of me. I will use my life knowledge, skills, and abilities to get out of this cave. If I can do that, I can definitely figure out a safe way to get out of this marriage. I'll need to be careful because I don't want to be harmed or killed by Sean or his family!

I untied my rope and latched it on a higher branch for stability. I mustered up all the strength I had left inside of me and slowly heaved my aching body out of the water. Just as I thought I had gripped on to the rock beneath me tightly enough, I slipped back into the water with a splash. *Come on, Kate! No more giving up.*

You're a fighter now! After two more failed attempts, I tugged hard on the rope with my raw hands to pull myself up out of the water. This time, I managed to not slip back down. I stabilized my footing and quickly scanned my surroundings. My backpack was within reach now, so I untied myself from the branch I'd tied my rope to. Slowly and carefully, I broke off a smaller branch from the fallen tree and extended the stick over the pool of water to catch my backpack strap. My first few attempts at reaching my backpack failed; I nearly slipped back into the water. *Please help me, God. I need you to guide me through this.*

Finally, I caught my backpack strap on the branch and delicately tugged the backpack towards me until it was within my reach. I said a quiet prayer to thank God for having helped me through this first step. Once my backpack was on my lap, I proceeded to pulling out dressings, tape, and antibiotic ointment to clean my abrasions. I felt a twinge as I began disinfecting my painful skin abrasions.

When I finished cleaning my wounds, I placed the dressings, wrappings and soiled swabs in my backpack. My stomach growled and cramped up from hunger. For once, I didn't want to eat simply to avoid my emotions, fears and frustrations. I was truly hungry. I reached into my backpack and pulled out a granola bar, carrots, an apple and a water bottle.

As I sipped the water and took my first bites of food, I realized that for the first time in a very long time, I actually enjoyed the taste of these foods. My parched lips cracked as I continued chewing the food. I shivered a bit less as I gained some of my strength back. My thoughts drifted off again. I went over in my mind all the times Sean had abused me emotionally. *My marriage is over and no religious nor societal values are going to keep me married to Sean anymore! I have a purpose in life – what exactly, I don't know yet. But it starts with leaving this marriage! ... Safely... I need to figure out how...*

I looked around me at the pit that I was in. I had hit rock bottom both literally and metaphorically. *The good news is: my life can only go uphill from here. No, life is not fair, but I can make different choices as I move forward, I could choose to say married to Sean. Or I could pluck up my courage and leave him. But I think I know very well now that the choice to stay married to him is no longer an option.*

A feeling of serenity came over my body. I felt deep within my gut that my life would improve – even if it took a long time. I could either choose fear or choose faith. It was up to me to decide. In that moment, I remembered my father telling me that as long as I truly believed in myself, I could find solutions to any of life's problems. The key was to keep moving forward. Answers would eventually come.

Perhaps this chapter in my life is just like traveling down a foggy road. I've got to keep driving in hopes that the fog will eventually lift. If I don't keep moving forward, in hopes of something better up ahead, I'll be stuck in the fog. I had lost my hope, which is why I was stuck on this foggy road. But I've got to keep on truckin'! Hope will get me through! I surprised myself with a laugh as I realized how I get out of this mess if I only believe in myself. It was though my renewed hope was already clearing up my vision on life that had been fogged up by Sean's emotional abuse. *I choose faith. I choose hope. I choose love. I decide to believe in a brighter future, in a life filled with purpose.*

I finished my snack, placed my food wrappers, apple core, empty water bottle into my backpack, and zipped it up. I looked up at the cave opening overhead. Suddenly it didn't seem so overwhelming anymore. My angel had returned and was watching over me. "Kate Louise," he exclaimed, "you found that hope is a key part of your solution. Now go find your steps for success. You are divinely protected!"

I gave him a big smile. "I am! Thank you! I

laughed and felt my rib cage ache from my fall.

He pointed to the way out of the dark cave, indicating that it was time to go. I turned around to pick up my backpack. When I turned back, he was gone again. I smiled, feeling warmth in my heart. *I've been loved this whole time. I've just been searching for love in the wrong places.*

I was determined to climb my way out of this cave, however hard it would be. *It's time to be strong and get on with my life!* My rope would be my lifeline to life. I lassoed my rope higher up around the fallen tree and then around bushes, higher up, placing one foot in front of the other carefully as I steadily climbed up the cave. The climb seemed never-ending. Every once in a while, I rested to catch my breath for a few minutes. Finally, I pulled my body up over the ledge I had fallen from and victoriously stood up, extending my hands up to the sky. *I did it! I really did it!* The sun warmed my icy cold cheeks. I took a few steps back from the ledge and peered down into the cave I had crashed down into. I gazed into the black pit as if I was looking back at my wasted years with Sean. *I climbed out of that like a true champion and*

I'll do the same with my marriage!

"Hello, sunshine!" I cried out joyfully. I studied the angling of the sun and determined that it must have been about 4 PM. My stomach growled loudly, but I knew I didn't actually want food. I was satisfied enough with my accomplishment. Wanting to savour the moment and to warm up my cold body, I sat on a big rock by the cave's opening, taking in the warm sunrays and fresh air.

Eventually, I secured my backpack, hooked my rope back to my body and zipped up my jacket. My spirit was revitalized with a new sense of determination. I wasn't certain what my next steps would be, but I knew that I would find my answers. I knew that my new life would be filled with love – I needed to look for it in the right places. I would surround myself with positive energy, loving people and uplifting activities. With my renewed excitement for life, I finally walked slowly back to the house.

When I arrived in the driveway, I was relieved

that Sean's car was nowhere to be seen. I quickly put away my backpack and my rope; I also threw away my soiled bandages and food scraps. After a warm shower, I sat down at my writing desk and turned on my computer. I felt energized, as if a flame was burning vibrantly in my soul. It was as though I had finally discovered a way to live happily and freely. While I didn't have all the answers as to how I would get out of my marriage, I knew that my life had changed into something wonderful. I wasn't worried, frustrated, or upset for the first time in a very long time.

Wow! We collected our clues which gave us an understanding of our anger and negative emotions. Are you surprised by what you wrote in your journal? I was when I read the above Kate's journal entry.

I wonder if we should do additional interviews, write in our diaries, or try another physical, spiritual or mindful opportunity. What do you want to do? Again, the choice is yours.

Understanding our interviews, we wonder about our next strategy to manage our anger and negative emotions. The answer is to dissolve our pain and our negativity by beginning a positive life fulfilling our true-life purpose, giving, and receiving love.

Do I hear you say why bother to dissolve this negativity to move to find our love? Do you remember that negativity can affect our minds, bodies, and spirits? These impacts may lead to stress, anxiety, illnesses, diseases, guilt, resentment, and the list continues. We do not want to carry those negativities, instead, let's do self-care known as our healing. One method of healing is to accept that we are human and made our mistakes. How do we proceed with this method?

To progress in our healing journey, we must restore our minds, bodies, and spirits with first loving ourselves and then other people. How do we regain our stable holistic being? Yes, our focus is on ourselves first. The restoration is not complicated, but it requires our time to renovate our precious mind, body, and spirit to love ourselves and others.

Oh, did I hear you said that 'I do love me.'

Really, my dear reader? Hmmm. My realization became aware that my self-love was missing. If I didn't love me, how could I expect other people to love me? This was a significant understanding. Do you agree? If not, why? Please allow yourself to wade through this loving, healing moment.

I soon realize that I must have self-love then I wonder how to do this strategy. The answers may include providing our bodies with proper nutrition, filling our minds with healthy thoughts, and having our spirits experience wholesome, healthy feelings.

Let's take a break from our investigation and love our minds, bodies, and spirits. Yes, you deserve to care for yourself. Please choose one or more ways to be kinder and loving towards yourself to include the following.

1. Sleep.

Sleep will improve your memory, rested body, and emotions with the simple act of sleeping. These benefits can't occur with the lack of sleep. Please consider if you are having a minimum of eight hours of sleep each day.

2.   Love.

Demonstrate loving yourself as you would a dear friend. Think and speak to yourself kindly. Your external friendships would never hurt other human beings by insulting them by saying they were fat, stupid, or ugly. Learn to accept all your flaws.

3.   Wake up with a positive attitude.

Say a chosen affirmation each morning. An example is: 'I am healthy, lovable, and function as a successful person today.'

4.   Write a letter.

Write a letter to yourself or the other person about what you identify, recognize, and understand how to heal your negative emotions. Once the letter is complete, please consider a simple ritual of releasing the negative feeling by sending it out into the universe. My method is that I burn the letter to rid myself of the negativity.

5.   Schedule a fun activity or day off.

Make an appointment on your calendar to enjoy yourself by reading a book, shopping, walking in the park, or anything that makes you smile. When you make an appointment, the anticipation is also a bonus to do one of the mindful, physical, or spiritual opportunities.

6.   Practice.

Another method is to practice some of your spiritual rites such as prayer, reading the religious documents such as the Christian Bible. These activities may change your negative passion into positive.

7.   Enjoy quietness.

Have a quiet moment alone is a treasure. The alone time is not to be feared, but a moment to improve your mind, body, and spirit by increasing your productivity, creativity, and clarity.

8. Say the word, 'no.'

The word no is a powerful word to meet your needs that considered are first. Yes, you can say it, 'no.' Otherwise, you and I have a desire to be superhuman to do it all. Right? Wrong!

9. Meditation.

Engaging in meditation is providing compassion and decreasing stress for your holistic being. The time can be as little as five minutes to an hour. The choice is yours.

10. Give kindness to others.

When you are kind to others, your heart feels love and promote your healing.

11. Change your to-do list.

When you look at your daily accomplishments, you will feel thankful for your life.

Please consider what are your priorities today and what tasks can wait until tomorrow. Why stress yourself out with a huge to-do list? Is it worth your anxiety? I think not.

12. Observe.

Observe how you talk about yourself and your past life. If you are like me in the grime, we spend a lot of time by complaining, gossiping, criticizing, blaming, and doubting. How can we take the time spent on these negative speaking styles to do something productive? Could you turn your speaking to positive thoughts about the other people and yourself?

13. Acceptance.

Accept that negative words and thoughts may stand up awkwardly, they are not entirely out of your mind as your pain will always be in presence in your mind, body, and spirit. Our goal is to manage the negativity rather than hide from it. Our successful healing depends on how we accept our negativity, handle it appropriately, turn it into a positive affirmation, and trust our intuition to move forward. Understand a negative thought is similar to a passing dark, stormy cloud which leaves to become a gorgeous rainbow.

14. Challenge.

Challenge yourself to manage your anger and negativity. Even negative views have no real focuses. Healing our pain can be challenging but may be calmer if your prompt to yourself by changing one thought at a time to positive. In an undetermined amount of time, you will notice that letting go of the anger and negative thoughts that free you to want to heal yourself.

14.   Forgive.

When you embrace yourself, love yourself, and forgive yourself, only then do you begin to heal your mind, body, and spirit. What is forgiveness? What is our understanding of forgiveness? Who do I forgive? When do I forgive? Where do I forgive? How do I forgive myself and others? Why do I want to heal my mind, body, and spirit? Let's go to the next chapter, 'The Time,' to learn how to forgive another person and yourself.

The Time

Since we have been undertaking the previous three strategies, our awareness exposes our desire to be free from our pain. I'm declaring it is *time* to release our anxiety and forgive the other person, yourself, or perhaps both. A sensible decision is to forgive by letting go of conflicting feelings about the other person who has hurt you.

Forgiveness is about releasing those negative emotions which may include anger, bitterness, and ideations of retaliation. Our strategy, forgiveness, is to reach into our mind, body, and spirit locating our empathy for the other person, ourselves, or perhaps both. Be aware that you do not have to minimize these harmful effects, but to forgive the appropriate individual. Let's proceed and answer the next questions about the act of forgiveness.

When we contemplate how to forgive, what do we know already? Let's quickly review our previous strategies. When we released our pain, the past three strategies discovered our daily expectations might not have met. They include your education, career, and relationships failing to achieve our goals causing our pain. This identified discomfort arose from a traumatic event such as developing health problems, divorce, injuries, the death of a loved one, and the list goes on. Do we hold our negativity or release it?

If we release our pain, what are the benefits to forgive? Some benefits include the release of cortisol levels harmful to our mental and physical health. Wanting to have these benefits, we study our multiple journal entries for clues for healing. During our review of past writings, we learn how to define our pain, anger, and negative emotions which may include disappointment, sadness, guilt, and anxiety. Additionally, we recognize our unstated rage which may have focused inward, at the other person, or both causing the pain to the other person or even ourselves.

Being caught up in our discomfort, we handled the traumatic event the best we know how. Our choices may be to deal with it directly, avoid managing the negativity, or deny the traumatic event occurred. I suggest that we take the direct, appropriate strategy known as, 'The Time." This moment is to work on this strategy, forgiveness, which decreases our cortisol levels which harms our physical body, spirit, and mind. Where do we forgive within our holistic being?

Look at your self-esteem which may have been injured. A considerable suggestion is to leave your self-esteem on the outside street. Yes, you and I know that we hold onto our negativity because our self-worth hurts. Putting our self-esteem aside, we can manage our anger and other negative emotions. Are you ready to begin? Yes? No? Maybe? Do you need time to consider this strategy? I'll wait for you, my dear reader.

How do we proceed with our healing? The process is similar to the previous three strategies by defining, recognizing, and collecting our clues about our forgiveness. This strategy may feel similar to our desire to run away like a frightened kitten who saw its image in a mirror. Sooner or later we become strong lions who want to declare freedom from our pain, to experience the act of forgiving the other person, ourselves, or both. Are you ready to explore forgiveness? Yes? No? Maybe? Please take a second or two to reflect if you will proceed.

Since we won't shy away from defining our forgiveness, it's time to do the next activity. Please pick up your pen to write or not. The choice is yours.

Activity #8

My definition of my forgiveness is…

What was your definition of forgiveness? The meaning of forgiveness may be to release our pain, our negative emotions, anger, and any less favorable core beliefs about ourselves, the other person, or perhaps both. The act of forgiveness may lead to identifying how we had placed blame on another person, or even ourselves. We don't want to accept a life sentence to live in pain by giving control to the event or the other person. We recognize the need to forgive.

Who do you forgive? Is there another person, yourself, or perhaps both? Forgiveness is a significant commitment, a wonderful gift to heal your mind, body, and spirit. It is also a difficult task to identify who is the focus on forgiveness especially if it is yourself. However, it is essential not to carry resentments; otherwise, we cannot live our true-life purpose. Shall we spend the time to clarify who the person to forgive? Do you want to journal, go for a walk, or talk to your love one to consider these questions? Again, the choice is yours. I'll be here waiting for your return.

Welcome back! Did you figure out who to forgive? Yourself? The other person? Or both? Now, ask can you put yourself in the other person's mind? Before we investigated our forgiveness, we paused, reflected, wrote, and felt our emotions, but now we must understand the other person. Can you figure out the reason the other individual treated you as they did? I'm not asking you to support their motives, consider why they acted as they did. Do you need time to journal? Yes? No? Maybe?

Did you find out who to forgive? No! Let's continue with your investigation by talking to your trusted family members or friend. During our conversations, we questioned our loved ones about their understanding of what happened. They may not have understood what happened, how wrong we felt, or inability to speak about our forgiveness plan.

Unable to share our forgiveness, we struggled within our spirits, bodies, and minds. Our spirits demand the freedom of the pain, but we can't find the solution. In comparison, our bodies may symbolize our skirmishes by either being overweight or underweight. Our minds feel heavy emotions of depression, guilt, or resentment. What do we do? Or are you thinking, why continue to do this strategy, healing?

Doing this method, you will develop a sense of being proud of yourself. Forgiveness is useful for healing yourself. As you continue to challenge yourself to look beyond all the less positive thoughts, ideas, and emotions, your healing will emerge from your mind, body, and spirit. Our action is to continue writing in our journals daily because we will soon discover the negativity slowly changes to positive thoughts. One of the diary entries may lead to the possibility to forgive at least that this happened to me.

When I journaled, my writings identified and recognized more details related to my pain. I wanted to quit journaling. Then, I soon grasped that I couldn't continue to write negative entries. I began writing positive words about my aspirations, dreams, and desires. My writing was a gift of self-love. It was as if the mind searched for beauty, discard the pain, and moved to a renewed life filled with love. Continuing to write, I pushed myself to go deep into my spirit and looked at forgiveness which I defined and recognized. Let's do it!

Each one of us will recognize forgiveness differently. Yes, my dear reader, we will spend some time analyzing forgiveness in the next activity. Why are you bothering to do this process? The reason is negativity may lead to harmful effects on our minds, bodies, and spirits which we described previously. Some additional harmful examples affect our holistic beings may include being distracted while driving carelessly, gaining weight, losing weight, and feeling depressed.

By pursuing forgiveness, we can accept the real-life gifts known as love, joy, happiness, peace, faith, and hope. Yes, it is time to pull out of our journals. I can hear your moans and protests but humor me. Let's recognize your ideal forgiveness.

Activity #9

My recognized forgiveness answers these questions:

1. What does forgiveness look like with myself or the other person?
2. Who do I forgive?
3. When does forgiveness occur?
4. Where does forgiveness take place?
5. How does forgiveness happen?

6. Why do I forgive the other person, myself, or both?

Are you surprised how you recognized your forgiveness or did you struggle? Will you be able to release your pain? Our painful situation will always be somewhere in our minds, bodies, and spirits, but forgiveness will lessen the negativity. How? Time is the successful key to our forgiveness based on the passage of moments decreases the negativity. It has a way for us to develop our understanding, empathy, and compassion for the other person, ourselves, or both. This process is not easy to do and can't be done in a minute or two.

Why? It is hard to recognize our involvement in our pain because if you are like me, then we blame the other person. Shall collect our clues about forgiveness by looking at our participation? Yes, we are going to pull out our journals for the next activity by going deep into your holistic being. Again, the choice is yours to proceed.

Activity # 10

Who did I blame? Myself or the other person?

Did you find any answers? Maybe not now, but later we may identify our involvement. Let's continue. Our identification is as we move towards our increased consideration of how our situation unfolded by giving ourselves understanding and empathy. We own our responsibility to provide our self-care, release the negativity, and forgive. The rationale is that we soon realize that benefits to forgiving as:

- Having a healthy mind, body, and spirit;
- Enjoying healthy relationships;
- Decreasing stress, fear, frustration, and doubt; and
- Increasing our time to focus on life's opportunities of love, joy, and happiness.

These benefits may expand as we continue to write in our journals. Yes, I am confident that you are saying, 'I can't write again.'

Remember, the purpose of our writing is to actively renew and redefine ourselves which will discover our true-life purpose. Our writing may reflect any of the chosen topics in our next activity. Yes, some of the writing may seem like repeated efforts, but you will go deeper and learn more about yourself. Let's go for it!

Activity #11

Please write about any or all of the following:

1. Acknowledge any negative emotions;
2. Recognize how negative emotions may affect your mind, body, and spirit;
3. Write about how holding your negativity will serve your true-life purpose;
4. Define your regrets related to your pain; or
5. Describe how you choose to forgive yourself, the other person, or both.

Did your journal give you some new insights? What are you feeling? I'm sure that you have some emotional responses. Let's dig deeper by stepping further down our path. The next powerful strategy is to describe a possible meeting with the other person, yourself, or both related to your forgiveness. We are not worried about their forgiveness.

Our next activity is to write what your forgiveness meeting looks like with the other person or yourself. If you cannot write, continue, and read Kate's journal. When finished thinking, reflecting, or reading, please join me after Kate's journal entry.

Activity #12

Describe your forgiveness meeting with the other person or yourself.

Kate's Journal:
Seeking Forgiveness

When I felt overwhelmed, I realized that it was time to forgive myself and my ex-husband. When? Where? How? I wish I knew the answers as I wrote in my journal.

Then, I received the dreaded phone call from my brother, Ben. He told me that Mom died.

Unaware of my next action, I felt prompted to phone my two brothers and my sister. I intended to invite him to come to my mother's calling hours at the funeral home. I wondered if my ex-husband would come and what would he say or do.

Success was seen as Claire, my sister, and both my brothers, Ethan and Ben, agreed to call Sean, my ex-husband.

Immediately, I went into overdrive by notifying my supervisor of my mother's death, rearranging my work schedule, reserving the airline tickets, ordering a rental car, and packing my suitcase.

Within those hours, I had also called my girlfriend, Mona Lies, to arrange a place to sleep. She agreed immediately.

While editing my college paper, I was struggling with many questions such as how should I approach him and what do I say? I saw the wall clock read 4:00 PM, and once again looked to my college paper.

Closing my computer, I walked away from my

oak desk and entered the bathroom. I showered, dried quickly with my blue towel, and applied my body deodorant. I dressed in a black dress, pulling on my dark stockings, matching black shoes.

While flying back to New York, I felt many tears fell upon my cheeks while thinking about our courtship, wedding, marriage, and divorce proceedings. Do I hug him? Who should offer a kiss or not? I felt more questions fly by my head similar to flying bullets from a machine gun.

When I arrived at the funeral home, I dreaded to open the huge oak front door. Abruptly, the front door swung open and the familiar funeral director, Mister White, emerged onto the porch. I recognized him. He was short, slightly overweight, red-checked, white hair and mustache.

"Welcome home, Kate Louise," he said, extending his right hand to shake mine.

"Ugh, thank you," I mumbled, looking down to the ground.

"Let me open the door for you, Kate Louise."

"Thank you, Mister White," I said, walking into the hallway, reading the sign on the right door,

'Ava L. Hill.' *Oh, it is real that Mom died.* I felt my weak knees buckle while my body lowered to the floor.

"Are you okay?" asked Mister White, reaching for me.

"Yes, I'll get my bearing,' I replied while I held his right arm to steady my balance. "Thank you."

"Do you want to go into your mother's room or sit down over here?" he asked, pointing to a blue chair in the corner.

"No, I'm fine," I said, sadly. "I want to see my mother."

"Her coffin is here to the right."

"Thank you." I walked slowly into the funeral parlor, seeing the silver-like coffin lined with various flower arrangements, smelling the familiar funeral home odors, tasting my blood on my tongue, hearing the soft classic background music, and finally feeling my mother's cold, pale hands.

Staring at the corpse, I could only think that this body couldn't be my mother. The stiff didn't even look familiar to me. I quietly bent my head forward and whispered a quiet prayer.

"Kate Louise, when did you arrive?" I turned to focus upon my sister's tearful face.

"I just got off the airplane, rented a car, and drove here immediately," I explained, "How are you, Claire?"

"I'm fine, I guess," she replied, wiping away a tear that rolls down her ashen face.

"How about a hug?"

"Yes," she said while we embraced and I felt the warmth of my sister's heart matching mine.

"Oh, look – Sean's here, "Claire announced when we separated from our loving hug.

I looked at Sean. *Boy, he's changed since our divorce proceedings!* I observed that he walked with an unfamiliar cane. I looked closer to see he had gained about fifty pounds and his black suit was too small.

I quickly walked to stand to his left. "Hello, Sean."

"Hello, Kate," he replied, lifted his walking cane, and began playing with it.

"We need to talk alone," I said without

realizing where those words came from my mouth.

"Yes."

"Let's find a private spot, Sean."

Out of nowhere, Mister White was at my side and directed us, "Follow me."

Sean and I walked to the private room on the left of my mother's room when the funeral director opened the door.

"Thank you, Mister White," I mumbled, walking into the smaller room.

"Your welcome, Kate Louise," he replied.

"Have a seat, Sean," I directed Sean to the overstuffed black chair while the funeral director closed the massive door.

Sean sat down and didn't speak a word.

"I want to talk without our lawyers, friends, or family members to speak for us."

"What do you want to talk about?" he asked in a soft, unfamiliar, anxious voice.

I continued, "I have a few questions that I want to ask. I am certain that you may have some questions also," I paused.

"Ask away," he replied, tilting his head downwards.

I promptly asked, "Do you love me?"

He didn't answer. *I feel like a fool and why did I ask for this meeting.*

My thoughts were interrupted when I heard Sean cleared his throat and inquired, "Was our sex satisfactory?"

I was shocked and sat there for a few minutes, I reflected on the other men with whom I shared intimate moments. Then, I said, "Yes, at that time it was."

He again played with his cane. Then, Sean stammered, "I guess that I should have paid more attention to you. I may have been wrong not to go to marriage counseling."

"I…I don't know what to say," I replied. "Did you love me?"

Hearing no response, I was aware of my anxiety with the quiet room for appropriately five minutes.

Suddenly, I heard my voice, "I now want to ask you a question, Sean. Can you forgive me since I broke our wedding vows until death do us part?"

I paused, took a deep breath, and continued, "I forgive you for your part in the failure of our marriage. I'm trying to forgive myself."

I watched Sean, and it seemed like forever before he spoke, "At this present time, I can't forgive you, but in time, I will forgive you, Kate Louise."

Then, he abruptly stood up.

I quickly stood up also and asked, "How about a hug?"

"Okay."

I slowly put my arms around him, but I didn't feel his. I felt his body was like a cold marble statue. I turned to his lips which he promptly turned his head away, and I didn't feel his arms around me.

"Gotta go."

I dropped my arms to my side and scrutinized Sean. He turned, moseyed slowly to the door, opened it, walked out, and closed the door. I, in turn, began-to cry, not realizing my sister, Claire, entered the room.

"Are you okay, Kate Louise?" she asked.

"Yes, I will be," I said, wiping away my tears,

"I just need to pull up myself and go forward."

"Where?"

"I don't know. I just know, but I will put one foot in front of the other," I sobbed.

My sister looked into my eyes and didn't speak.

"I'll figure the location in time," I said, feeling her warm embrace while my tears raced like sleds down a slippery hill. *How can I forgive me? I forgave Sean; therefore, I forgive me. I need to believe my words.*

I felt Claire put her loving arms tighter around me and I did the same. I cried while she held me.

Welcome back! If you read Kate's journal, the entry was on the actual time I met my ex-husband. My two goals included giving and receiving forgiveness because I spend time writing about this meeting answering my questions: who, what, when, why, where, and how. The meeting was not what I had envisioned; however, it gave me closure to our divorce and answered my prayers to my higher spirit, God.

When we define and recognize forgiveness, we soon realize that forgiveness is beyond our holistic being. How? Forgiveness involves our spiritual beliefs whether the mystical essence is Buddha, Father, God, Holy Spirit, and the list goes on. You and I need not have the same spiritual guide; however, I am sure each one of us has one.

Within our higher spirits, we reach for the love which will make it easier to face the wrongs honestly by the other person, ourselves, or both. The successful goal is not to judge anyone harshly, but it is to release our negativity and find gratitude for the lessons learned.

We will need time to heal by examining what forgiveness is. I suggest journaling, thinking, reflecting, or talking to someone who loves you. Someone who has no expectations and listens to you. These activities include to preserve your life's passionate force, to forgive, and do not carry the pain inside your mind, body, and spirit. While we studied our past, we understand that we can't undo it and our life happened. We come to terms to accept the past which our acceptance leads to healing.

If we could re-do our past, we appreciate that we could make another choice. However, the new decision is on today's knowledge. This discovery is our assertion we not only learned from our pain, but we understand what new knowledge, abilities, and skills gained from that experience, our pain.

Our understanding expands the realization we did the best we could do at the time of our pain. The methods we used depended upon our knowledge we had, the amount of life experience, and how we were supposed to manage our sadness at the moment.

Knowing these details, we soon realize that we must give ourselves a break and say thank you to our younger selves for the management of our painful event. While we understand these positive efforts, we soon discover our regrets.

Our regrets often take more time and effort for us to understand the past. Please allow yourself to feel them by journaling. In time, you will find your acceptance, understanding the pain, and you did the best at the moment of time. While journaling, let your pen repeat and repeat some of the writing about your pain. I believe you will sooner or later be ready to move on, accept the past, understand the history made who you are, be thankful for the pain, and truly forgive yourself.

Eventually, you have the choice of how you proceed through this healing journey by following your intuition. You can manage any of your future situations which may be confusing and challenging. However, you slowly want to find your true-life purpose and, on the clarity, how to achieve your healthier mind, body, and spirit while you expand your forgiveness. Slowly, we look beyond the pain because it no longer serves as our true-life purpose. You will begin to ask the question, why am I here?

Searching for the answer to this question, why am I here, you may learn of the other people who you are now respecting, being compassionate, and demonstrate empathy. Understanding you are healing and living your life passion, please ask yourself if your daily decisions are a part of your true-life purpose. Yes? No? Maybe?

Is it time to do a physical, mindful, or spiritual opportunity to relieve stress? Please do so. Thanks!

An overview of these past four strategies, we understand that a crime, our pain, occurred. If there was no pain or crime, then we would have no healing journey to travel. However, we discovered that our suffering was the cause of our negative emotions including anger which we refused to feel during the traumatic event. Our pain could be huge as a death, or as small as an offensive glare.

These painful situations may not have been that origin us to hurt, but rather how we understand it. Now we decide to forgive and move forward to discover our true-life purpose in our final strategy, 'The Prime.'

The Prime

Our lives may be filled with many successful keys to include strength, courage, faith, love, and happiness used to define our prime, the true-life's purpose. Our strength is to get up in the morning and face adversity. Our courage is seen as going forward into the unknown day. Our faith is our inner, hot flame looking to the higher spirit whether it's God, Buddha, or another spiritual guide for guidance to discover our true-life purpose. Our love and happiness are the two motivators for managing our true-life purpose.

How do we define our true-life purpose?

'I don't know,' you may have replied.

I understand you don't know. I'm still exploring my true-life purpose by continuing to answer the six detective questions: who, what, when, where, why, and how. Are you willing to explore those questions again?

Perhaps you are feeling overwhelmed and

frustrated that we asked yet again those darn questions. Maybe you realized those answers reflected our life events such as our youth, college, career, marriage, children, divorce, and our aging process. Or do you need more time to reflect on each event in your journal? Yes? No? If so, I will wait for your return.

Activity #13

1. What is my true-life purpose?
2. When will I begin my true-life purpose?
3. Where do I serve my true-life purpose?
4. How I implement my true-life purpose?
5. Why do I do my true-life purpose?
6. Who will benefit from me serving my true-life purpose?

Did you struggle with answering these questions? Please consider some concepts that related to our true-life purpose. Our lives reveal the true-life purpose of what we experience in our struggles, frustrations, and even annoyances. You may ask the opposite by questioning what I do enjoy in life-related moments such as work, hobbies, conversations, and research. What are yours? Do you want to journal answering these considerations? Again, the choice is yours.

Let's use our process as would a detective examines our prime known as the true-life purpose. The sleuth finds these answers by stepping backward. How do we move back? Hmmm. Pause for a minute to look at your life at this very moment by doing another activity.

Activity #14

Please answer these questions:
1. How do you live each moment?
2. How do you spend your time?
3. What do you enjoy doing each day?
4. Who do you spend your time with?
5. Why?

6. When do you love yourself or the other person?

7. What is your future true-life purpose?

8. Did I hear something filled with anger, negativity, or a flash of a bad memory from your pain?

9. Are you complaining, grumbling, bitching, or saying negativity about your life?

10. Stop! Did we go through the four strategies: crime, slime, grime, and time?

11. Did we not release the anger and the other negative emotions?

12. Is there more negativity to release?

13. Do you need more time to forgive yourself or another person further?

14. What else do you need to do?

You may even find you need to go back one more time to study those darn four past strategies yet again. You may want to reflect on the four strategies, 'The Crime, Slime, Grime, and Time!' Please know it is not shameful to return to one of the strategies. Realize the traveling on this healing journey is not a day to read this book. It may take you a long time.

Did I hear you gasp? Yes, I took over ten years to come to this understanding. I cannot give you an estimated amount of time, neither will you.

Reflect for a few minutes to consider what is your next strategy. Do you need to rethink a previous strategy? I'll wait for you. The choice is yours.

Welcome back! Now, my dear reader, I invite you to walk into your purpose. Yes, we can together. Can you humor me for this last strategy? I imagine that you are tired, frustrated, and feel when are we going to find our true-life purpose?

First, look again at your past writings in your diary. Our writing and investigations are meaningful by spending so much effort, sweat, and tears. Yes, those darn tears kept coming especially when we mourned our past and even present lives. These powerful moments spread from sorrow pits to mountain tops of happiness, joy, love, and peace. Did you read anything in your journal that spoke about your true-life purpose?

I believe that you will find your sweet moments in your life that reflect your positive thoughts and actions. Maybe you are like me while questioning myself and ask how would I have been so stupid?

The truth was in those happy moments. We soon realize our positive actions reflected something so elementary that we give a tap on our forehead. What is our true-life purpose? I think that we finally have the answer first to accept and love our younger selves who made the best decision at the time of our traumatic event.

Yes, you read to accept and love yourself. I'm also requesting you recognize your past decisions were made based on the information you had back then. Yes, we can make better decisions because we have more information now. You did not make wrong choices.

However, let's decide to do the next strategy to discover our true-life purpose, 'the Prime.' Every strategy of this journey has meaning even those strategies that seem to be in reverse. Those strategies are important. Why? I am trying to answer that question, and you also have struggled to find the solution. However, our progression moves forward to consider what is our true-life purpose.

What do we do now? When we continue to look for our true-life purpose, you and I are creating it. How? We decided whether to spend time worrying if we make the right decision for the current action or not.

If you are like me, worry fills your heart and wonder if your choice is the right one. Creating the courage to step forward is somehow related to living at this moment, not the past, or future. It may be frightening, but our lives will improve.

Where is the support for our decision? My support is that I trust in the higher spirit which may be defined as God, Buddha, or some higher spirit whose name is unknown. My higher spirit, God, guides me to make the right decision. Our decisions may be not including to step forward, to go backward, or to make no choice.

Oh, did I hear that you question whether a no choice is a decision? Yes! Sadly, if we refused to make a choice, we are setting a trap we won't be able to live our true-life purpose. Your question may be what do I do, Anne?

The choice is to think about what to do is and realize that change is inherent in our lives. Please understand the reason you refuse to change may be due to fear. Lean forward and trust because once fear removed, then we can devote our focus on the chosen true-life purpose.

Yes, I fear the unknown, but my attention is to serve my true-life purpose by writing this book. I now realize that I can speak and not hide behind Kate. I appreciated that my intuition showed my true-life purpose. Are you ready to focus on your intuition to discover your true-life purpose? Yes? No?

When you and I genuinely follow our intuition, we have a clearer understanding to listen to our appropriate decisions in our everyday life. How do we know if we are making the appropriate decision? I tune into my body's response when I ask a simple question answered with 'yes' or 'no.' The 'yes' answer feels lighter in my soul. Then, I know that I made the right decision and can continue to focus on my true-life purpose.

Your focus will be taking those cautious strategies forward, and your higher spirit will guide, protect, and provide knowledge how to proceed with your true-life purpose. In this belief, you and I will crawl, walk, run and even fall as we pursue our true-life purpose. How?

I am laughing because we will ask those six darn questions again. Are you ready?

Activity #15

Please write in your journals to answer the six darn questions plus two more! Thank you.

1. Who are you?

2. Where are you?

3. How do you see your true-life purpose?

4. What is your true-life purpose?

5. What do you love to do?

6, When will you take your step forward
towards your true-life purpose?

7. Why did you want to heal your mind,
body, and spirit?

8. Finally, have you found love on this
journey?

What did you learn from your
journaling? I learned to share my lessons
learned and found my answers. My answers
led me to my true-life purpose. Yes, I think
you realize my life purpose was to write this
book and 'talk' to you. Writing this book, I
shared my knowledge, skills, and abilities to
live and embrace a positive, guilt-free lifestyle
filled with love, joy, happiness, and peace.

What is yours, my dear friend? I
believe you can discover your true-life
purpose. Please go out and live your life to the

fullest. May we have the opportunity to meet. I hope so. Good luck!

Conclusion

Wow! Have you found the answer to our question, why heal your mind, body, and spirit? Did you discover your true-life purpose? Yes, I am confident that you have these answers.

I also believe that you will continue the healing of your mind, body, and spirit! The reason is you want to sooner or later further investigate by defining, recognizing, collecting clues, discovering your true-life purpose, and finding love for yourself and others.

How do you continue your investigation? I recommend that you set short and long-term goals by examining your passion, brainstorm your opportunities, ask questions, and go confidently into your future by these nine suggestions.

The first suggestion is to get out of your way. How do you get out of your way? What do you block the achievement of your daily and long-term goals? Is a lack of self-belief that you can do it? Is the problem Due to the lack of time, money, or motivation? Please consider removing your block by reflecting and journaling for the solution.

Second, stop delaying taking the first step. Why are you waiting? Please consider living today as your last day. Would this thought motivate you to act?

Next, ask what daily actions you will take? Will you write an email, dial the phone, or visit the customer, your friend, co-worker, or family member? The choice is yours. Do it! Time is decreasing, right?

Oh, your action failed. What will you do? No action is a choice, but it is ineffective. Why not consider, if it doesn't work, do something else. Some examples may include writing a letter, delivering a flower, or saying a thank you.

Number five is not to be upset about your mistake. What did I say? I am requesting that you understand maybe it was a mistake and figure out how to manage it more effectively next time. Get going and try again. I know you must pull on your inner strength because I believe you have it. Otherwise, why are you reading these words?

The sixth method is to rest when tired. I recognize that you may say that you don't have time to rest. However, your body, mind, and spirit may need to energize. Please know that it isn't wasted time.

Or maybe you can give love? Yes, you can share love to others which may include your family, friends, neighbors, co-workers, and the list continues. Why keep love locked in your heart?

Number eight is to live your life without blaming others. The action is seen as you accept your responsibility for your actions. Sometimes it is challenging to accept your responsibility when the move seems to be a failure. However, please look at the satisfaction understanding it. Is it not worth trying? I think it is.

Finally, I encourage you to continue to do one of the golden opportunities for your mind, body, and spirit to love your holistic being daily.

Yes, my dear reader, do you want to know my answer to the question, why heal your mind, body, and spirit is? Drum roll…The simple answer is the way that we live a wonderful life filled with peace, love, joy, and happiness. These successful answers reveal your true-life purpose.

Living your beautiful purpose embraces your healthy mind, body, and spirit by releasing forgiveness and loving others and yourself. How? The method is to engage at this very moment by participating in every action! Go forward into your precious lives with love similar to my delightful image of a little raindrop.

My beautiful image is a tiny waterdrop who travels through its life which is comparable to our lives. The little waterdrop arrives during a soft, gentle rain, and lands in a mud puddle in a small country lane. It feels protected in this insignificant water source until a big truck tire splashes it into a nearby stream. Our little droplet lands in a small stream and travels gently down the waterway until it arrives in a small pond.

Our little waterdrop jumps and swims around the pond with the anticipation of its bright future. Suddenly it sees the mouth of the large river feeling its curiosity as to where does this water lead into the big expanding world. While going down the river, the little waterdrop is riding the dangerous rapids, hitting against the rough rocks, swirling around the whirlpool, being thrown against the shore, trying to swim in safe waters, and struggling to get back into the midstream.

After dealing with all river events, the waterdrop arrives in a peaceful ocean and believes that its old age is going be easy and smooth sailing. However, it frequently swims into the ocean and soaks the sun rays until the ominous clouds, lightning bolts, and loud thunderclaps arrive.

Fearing a pending rainstorm, the small waterdrop swims ashore while it tossed, jerked around, and struck by the unexpected lightning bolt. Its skirmishes around as the realization is the little waterdrop caught up in the hurricane, and it wonders what will happen? Could I have lived my life better? I wonder…

The moral of the story is our experiences are similar to the little raindrop. As our arrival from our mother's wound, being thrown into our childhood and teenage years. Then, we enter into the main river, to enter college and to emerge into our chosen careers. While our work lives become involve, our personal lives participate rapidly in our home responsibilities, getting married, buying our homes, having children, welcoming grandchildren, and retiring. Suddenly, we realize that we are old, and facing our deaths. While we do our life reviews, we may question if we have served our true-life purposes.

I believe that we indeed live our true-life purposes filled with the abundance of love, joy, happiness, and peace. I know this is a fact that you are living to the fullest.

I wish you blessings with your continued exploration of your true-life purpose and healing of your healthy mind, body, and spirit. Understanding your true-life purpose as written by C.S. Lewis, 'you can't go back and change the beginning, but you can start where you are, and change the ending.'

TOOLKITS

Relaxing Breathing Exercises

While managing the healing of our painful life crises, we may feel stress affecting our minds, bodies, and spirits. Defining our stress level, we recognize that the need to manage our stress because multiple adverse effects may occur as:

- Increased blood pressure
- Headaches
- Stomach ulcers
- Pain in any part of our body
- Depression
- Premature Aging of our bodies
- Weight Gain or Loss
- Sadness
- Anxiety
- Hopelessness
- Any other adverse impact on our minds, bodies, and spirits.

Understanding how stress can affect our

minds, bodies, and spirit, we look for stress reduction methods. One method may include selecting one of the one hundred and fifty-six suggestions listed in the back of this book or fifty-two ideas for mind, body, and spirit

Additionally, I include the method known as the relaxing breathing. The goal of relaxing is to decrease our stress because it is free, can be done at any time, and any place. The reason I chose breath is it also can manage the fight or flight responses.

When stressing about our painful life crises, our bodies cope with either fight or flight responses. Fight responses may include anger and agitation which can be a useful response to lifesaving emergencies when we must act immediately. A flight example is our child crosses the street while an approaching car is driving too fast. We grab our child out of the car's dangerous path. Our bodies respond to the strength of our arms and legs to move and carry the child out of danger. However, our bodies can wear down, affect our minds negativity, and depress our spirits under the daily stress of dealing with our painful life situations.

In comparison, our flight reactions may be depressed and withdrawn when we think about our pain. These reactions may tear on our minds, bodies, and spirits to age prematurely such as decrease function to our mental responses, physical moments, and sad moods. We also lose way from our serving our true-life purpose.

Doing the breathing, we will realize these benefits:

- Decreased heart rate,
- Increased energy,
- Lessen our fears and frustrations,
- Deeper and slower breathing,
- Prevent the potential of having a disease,
- Lower blood pressure,
- Have less or no bodily pain,
- Increase problem solving,
- Have more motivation,
- Upsurge blood flow to our brain.

These benefits provide positive effects upon of minds, bodies, and spirits. Our minds are not filled with sadness, depression, and being withdrawn whereas these negative moods can affect our bodies as to our eating, sleeping, exercising, and socializing daily routine. Since our minds and bodies are in negative frames, then our spirits are also going into a depression. Somehow and someday we realize that we must figure out a method to reverse our stress which today we choose to do relaxing breathing. How? The deep relaxing breath is uncomplicated by these strategies:

1. Either stand or sit in a comfortable spot with a straight erect position.
2. Breathe deep from your stomach which you can feel the depth by placing your hand on it.
3. Feel the fresh air enter into your lungs which you can put your opposite hand on your chest.
4. Inhale again from your stomach.
5. Exhale slowly through your mouth pushing out the air as you contract your stomach.
6. Repeat for at least three cycles of inhaling and exhaling.

Tips for Successful Journaling

Did you journal a diary when you were a teenager? I think you may have as I did. When we had our precious journals, we often shared our deep, dark secrets, fears, frustrations, anxieties, and dreams. Upon completion of our entries, we would hide our secret journals under the mattress, dresser drawer, or closet.

When we graduate from high school, we declared that our journaling would stop as we were now adults. We didn't recognize the benefits of journaling as to the following:

- Decrease stress
- Lower depression
- Improve our emotions
- Manage our anxieties
- Clarify our problems, fears, and frustrations.

Initially, I'm sure you, like me, didn't

understand the value of our journals. If you have an old diary, please read it. Our journaling reflected how we defined our problems, recognized how it affected, and documented our emotions. An example of our writing may have revealed a possible teenage problem, the lack of attention from a good-looking boy. We would continue writing about how we saw our response to him and his response. Does this procedure sound familiar?

May I encourage you to journal daily for a few minutes or longer. I would give you this suggestion for successful journaling:

1. Begin with the desire to write in your journal. Oh, I know you may face days you have no hope. These days are most important to journal something.

2. Schedule time to journal daily for as little as five minutes. Yes, I am suggesting scheduling on your calendar. Ideally, the time is at a minimum of thirty minutes to an hour.

3. Have your pen and paper, a notepad, or a computer readily available.

4. To begin journaling, consider writing the date and time. Later, you may want to know the date and time of your entry.

5. Write in your style because no one will be editing your journal. I called this freestyle writing or an open mind. Your pen may find its own words! Mine did.

6. Share your journal if you desire or not. Remember the choice is yours.

7. One golden suggestion is to write as if you wrote to a dear friend. This method will reflect your honest, truthful, and open communication of your true feelings, fears, and frustrations. Yes, I can state honestly to write this way.

8. Allow your writing to reflect negative emotions which will slowly move to positive ones.

9. Answer those six detective questions as the following:

    a. Who was involved?
    b. When did it occur?

c. What happened?

d. Where was it?

e. How was it happening to you, or the other person, or both?

f. Why did it happen?

10. Simply enjoy writing and just let the words speak for you. I discovered such freedom. My desire is you find yours!

Mind Opportunities

Please select one of the one hundred and fifty-six opportunities to relieve the stress and give love to our minds, bodies, and spirits. These fifty-two opportunities are offered separately for the mind, body, and spirit by loving our holistic beings. Let's begin with some mindful opportunities.

1. Discuss your thoughts on new development in your community.
2. Understand your fears when you journal.
3. Overcome your anxieties when you talk to another person.
4. Journal daily.
5. Talk to your pet and watch its signs of love to you.
6. Smile.
7. Pack a lunch and enjoy driving on a new road.
8. Learn a new language such as Polish, Swedish, Danish, etc.

9. Study a new subject unrelated to your familiar career.

10. Write a paper on a new topic.

11. Think positive.

12. Read a drama novel or informative magazine about cooking, gardening, etc.

13. Watch a live theater production.

14. Try out for an acting audition.

15. Be focus on this present moment of joy, love, peace, and happiness.

16. Allow your emotions to occur and let them float away like clouds. You don't have to pay attention to them all.

17. Do a crossword puzzle.

18. Complete a zulucko.

19. Enjoy sex.... hmm.... I think you may see this opportunity again! LOL.

20. Enjoy a conversation with a dear friend or family member over a cup of coffee.

21. Go on vacation.

22. Savor the moment with no thoughts and enjoy the quietness.
23. Help someone with a simple task.
24. Pay for someone's coffee or meal.
25. Spend time looking at old photos.
26. Take new pictures.
27. Paint with oils.
28. Do arts and crafts. An example is to work with clay.
29. Write your autobiography.
30. Quit unhealthy habits such as smoking and excessive alcohol.
31. Drive a different route home.
32. Shop in a new store.
33. Try an original recipe you found on the Internet.
34. Create a scrapbook.
35. Surf the Internet and read a new website.
36. Talk to a stranger at the coffee shop.
37. Look at an object and think of a new use for it.

38. Create a new recipe from your favorite ingredients without following a cookbook.

39. Borrow a new book from the local library.

40. Offer assistance to an older person who lives alone. They may need help with changing a light bulb.

41. Listen to your loved one tell their pain.

42. Adopt a pet.

43. Seek a professional therapist as necessary.

44. Have your doctor readjust your prescriptions and review your over the counter supplements.

45. Try new spices and herbs in your food.

46. Evaluate your food intake for new habits.

47. Evaluate and try new flavors for your caffeine, sodas, water, and alcohol.

48. Watch a dramatic movie.

49. Walk the shore of a pond, river, or ocean.

50. The next time you are asked to do something and you don't want to do it, please say, 'No.' Be free to do the life activities you want to enjoy!

51. Listen and don't talk for twenty-four hours. I learned a lot when I did this opportunity!

52. Do you remember one of your youthful dreams? Can you do it now? Why not? Go forward and do it! I dare you... LOL

Body Opportunities

Please select one of the fifty-two opportunities to relieve the stress and give love to our bodies. Let's continue with some physical opportunities.

1. Go for a walk in your favorite outside place such as the park, ocean, or woods in the warm sunshine.

2. Eat a fresh fruit such as an apple, banana, orange, etc., to savor the natural sugar.

3. Sip fresh water which will decrease our desire for excess food.

4. Spoil yourself by going out for a meal with a friend, family member, etc., to reconnect in their love for you.

5. Sleep for eight hours and feel refreshed.

6. Do a hike longer than a walk to increase your body's ability to function.

7. Select a new flavor from your favorite beverage such as coffee, tea, or alcohol

to wake your taste buds.

8. Consider yourself like a king or queen who makes healthy choices for the leanest to fattest for protein: fish, poultry, pork, or beef.

9. Exercise a different type activity each day. Examples may include walking, jogging, dancing, working out in a water aerobics class, etc.

10. Take a deep inhale and exhale each hour while awake.

11. Ride a bike on a beautiful nature path.

12. Manage your stress by looking at how you spend your time.

13. Eat healthy nuts such as almonds.

14. Sample a different cultural food.

15. Enjoy a glass of wine.

16. Get a body massage.

17. Have a pedicure.

18. Enjoy your fingernails being painted a new color.

19. Obtain a new hairstyle.

20. Laugh at silly jokes.

21. Dance – any style you desire!

22. Feel the pain and manage it – pain medications as the last choice. Instead, I would recommend listening to a guided visualization on YouTube.

23. Eat a meatless green salad before your main course and savor the vegetables.

24. Evaluate and adjust your eating habits to be mindful. Are you eating without thinking? Late night eating? Are you skipping breakfast or another meal? Why?

25. How fast are you eating? Are you savoring your foods? Are you eating a meal in less than twenty minutes?

26. Eat a healthy breakfast – don't skip it.

27. Consider reducing the size of your plate then you won't feel deprived.

28. Recognize your taste choice as either sweet or salty when you feel stressed. Can you do something else to reduce your stress?

29. Enjoy sex…smiling!

30. Monitor amount of alcohol consumed – do you drink too much?

31. Relax in an Epsom salt bath.

32. Try aromatherapy.

33. Choose healthy side servings. Think about your selections related to fat, sodium, and calorie count.

34. Don't be tempted by the bowls of chips, peanuts, rolls, or fried Chinese noodles. Ask yourself if the food item is worth the mindless nibbling to add extra calories, fat, or sodium.

35. Go on vacation and enjoy learning about a new culture.

36. Go nude while doing your house cleaning. Why not?

37. Dress up in sexy clothes.

38. Consider adding fruit and removing high caloric food such as bacon, cheese, croutons, or bread chunks from your salad.

39. Have new makeup done at the local department store.

40. Replace your perfume with a new one and toss out the old. Why keeps memories? Hmmm…

41. Buy new underwear and bra which you may feel like a new person.

42. Swim laps.

43. Ask for a doggie bag when ordering your meal. Why eat the excess calories? It will be a great lunch tomorrow!

44. Consider ordering an appetizer as main entry.

45. Make faces in your mirror and love you!

46. Pat your back.

47. Play a card game.

48. Engage in a tennis match.

49. Bite into fresh raw vegetables such as carrots, radishes, and celery.

50. Daydream – hey, it's in your head. I'm not sure what but make your daydream

wonderful!

51. Love your pet or your neighbor's pet.

52. Send me an email of some idea that you came up to stimulate your mind @ **gps.9339@gmail.com** I am very curious what was your opportunity!

Spirit Opportunities

Please select one of the fifty-two opportunities to relieve the stress and give love to our spirits. Let's continue with some spiritual opportunities.

1. Attend a spiritual service such as church.
2. Enjoy the sunset and listen to nature for the night's rest.
3. Be grateful and write daily in your journal about five things you are thankful for.
4. Buy a house plant and care for it once a week. Two examples include watering the plant or pruning off the dead leaves.
5. Adopt a pet. An example may include a dog or cat.
6. Do yoga.
7. Practice daily meditation by listening to a guided one on YouTube.
8. Sit and absorb a beautiful sunrise.

9. Study a beautiful rosebud and see all the colors.

10. Ground yourself by walking barefoot in the grass or sand.

11. Spend time with your loved ones and put away the electronics such as a computer or iPhone.

12. Learn about a new religion.

13. Write out painful memories and then burn them. The act of scorching the memories is a form of releasing them.

14. Identify your core values in your journal and revisit them yearly. I think you will be surprised that they change.

15. Dance in the moonlight and howl.

16. Have an enjoyable sex encounter. Need I say more? LOL.

17. Enjoy walking around the house nude and no cleaning this time!

18. Say a chant. Yes, your song need not have sensible words.

19. Pray to your spiritual being.

20. Go on vacation even if it is going a couple of hours away from your home.
21. Have a good cry. Don't worry they are not crocodile tears.
22. Laugh! Yes, laugh!
23. Claim your willpower to manage any bad habits such as overeating, excess shopping, drinking, etc.
24. Pretend you have the energy and do something.
25. Study your passions and examine them as they related to your true-life purpose.
26. Visit with an older person in a nursing home, private home, assisted living or independent facility. They would love to share a conversation.
27. Encourage a younger person for their future endeavors. Do you remember your mentor who encouraged your future plans? It felt good, right?
28. Mentor a student for their hard class.

29. Love your life for the simple things such as your home, your friends, or your family.
30. Believe in yourself. Oh, I know this opportunity is hard but worth it!
31. Be mindful in your daily life activities such as washing dishes, making your bed, etc.
32. Sing with the radio, YouTube, etc....it feels good.
33. Be optimistic about anything and everything.
34. Be an inquisitor and ask those six darn questions. You know...who, what, where, where, why, and how.
35. Show compassion to yourself and others.
36. Rid yourself of toxic relationships – ask is it worth keeping those people around and draining your life force?

37. Get a new job – Please weigh your pros and cons when making this decision.
38. Volunteer – the benefits are outstanding for helping others.
39. Do something daring such as skydiving.
40. Set up a Facebook account and connect with old friends. If you have a Facebook account, search for old friends from high school, colleges, or old jobs.
41. Write a letter to your future self. What you do tell yourself about today? Or what would your future person tell you about your future?
42. Write a thank you note to a loved one. Or a strange twist is to write a thank you note to yourself.
43. Daydream about your next vacation, weekend, etc.
44. Plan a social event such as a luncheon for your friends.

45. Join an organization matching your talents such as writing, knitting, sharing a breakfast, etc.
46. Clean a closet shelf or a drawer.
47. Go thrift shopping and enjoy finding your items.
48. Prepare a home-cooked meal and set a beautiful table with flowers.
49. Choose a physical activity you never did before. An example may be dancing the fox-trot.
50. Sleep in your favorite bed or swing.
51. Cuddle up with your favorite blanket and share a conversation with a loved one.
52. Love yourself.

References

AZ Quotes. C.S. Lewis Quotes. Retrieved June 24,
2018, from
http://www.azquotes.com/quote/1334084

*Choosing to Forgive: Therapeutic Stages of
Forgiveness.*
Laura Chang (2017). Retrieved December 31,
2017 from
**https://www.mindfulnessmuse.com/positive
- psychology/choosing-to-forgive-
therapeutic-steps-of-forgiveness**

*Give and Take: Why Helping Others Drives Our
Success,* Grant Adams (2014). Retrieved
December 3, 2017 from
**https://www.amazon.com/Give-Take-
Helping-Others-
Success/dp/0143124986/ref=sr_1_1?s=book
s&ie=UTF8&qid=1512312692&sr=11&key
words=give+and+take+adam+grant**

How to Handle People Who Have Betray You, D.C.
McAllister. (October 3, 2016). Retrieved
December 3, 2017 from
http://thefederalist.com/2016/10/03/handle-people-betray/

11Important Life Lessons Enrich Soul (August 25,
2017). Retrieved August 26, 2017, from
http://www.viralnovelty.net/11-important-life-lessons-enrich-soul/

Jacinto, G.A., and Edwards, B. L. (2011). Therapeutic
Stages of Forgiveness and Self-Forgiveness.
*Journal Human Behavior in the Social
Environment,* 21, p. 423-437.

Logan, A. M. (2016) Where Are You? Search for the
Truth. Wilmington, N.C. Grow Power Self
Improvement, LLC

Logan, A.M. (2015) Who Are You? Planned Escape
from Abuse. Wilmington, N. C.

Pratt, Kim. (February 3, 2014). *Psychological Tools: What is Anger? A Secondary Emotion* Retrieved April 8, 2018, from **https://healthypsych.com/psychology-tools-what-is-anger-a-secondary-emotion/**

Six Steps to Control Your Emotions, Dr. Carmen Harra. (2017). Retrieved October 12, 2017, from **https://www.huffingtonpost.com/dr-carmen-harra/controlling-your-emotions_b_3654326.html/**

10 Ways to Forgive Yourself & Let Go of the Past. Megan Hale (October 29, 2013). Retrieved June 24, 2018, from **https://www.mindbodygreen.com/0-11454/10-ways-to-forgive-yourself-let-go-of-the-past.html**

10 Quotes from the Fearless Arianna Huffington. Grace Reader (2018). Retrieved June 24, 2018, from ***https://www.entrepreneur.com/article/279062***

13 Steps to Recover from Betrayal, Dr. Carman Harra. (2017). Retrieved December 3, 2017, from **https://www.huffingtonpost.com/dr-carmen-harra/14-steps-to-recover-from-_b_5660057.html**

13 Steps to Recover from Betrayal, Dr. Carman Harra. (2017). Retrieved December 3, 2017, from **https://www.huffingtonpost.com/dr-carmen-harra/14-steps-to-recover-from-_b_5660057.html**

20 Essential Truths That Women Over Fifty Wants to Share with Younger Women. Fran Sorin (October 31, 2017). Retrieved December 29, 2017, from https://www.huffingtonpost.com/entry/20-essential-truths-that-women-over-50-want-to share_us_587f561fe4b0b110fe11dc3e?ncid=tweetlnkushpmg00000050

About the Author

Anne M. Logan, MSN, MHSA, BSN, RN is currently the Manager of Grow Power Self Improvement, LLC. Her nursing practice includes forty plus years in various healthcare settings and community colleges where she held different nursing roles. Ms. Logan has self-published two fictional, inspirational, and self-help novels, <u>Who Are You? Planned Escape from Abuse</u> and, <u>Where Are You? The Search for Truth</u>. Now she has self-published the non-fiction known as <u>Why Heal Your Mind, Body, and Spirit? Sleuthing Ways to Love</u>. Ms. Logan is currently a healthcare consultant, author, and lecturer.

Value Your Feedback

Do you love this book? Do you have comments or questions? Or do you want the author, Anne M. Logan, to come to speak to your group?

We'd love to hear from you! Our valued readers are our top priority. Please go to the website, **https://gpsanne.com** to send a note. We'll make every effort to respond promptly. Thank you.